G000245832

SARK

A Feudal Fraud ?

by

Peter J Rivett

ISBN 0-9534947-2-1

Published by
Planetesimal©Publishing Limited
PO Box No. 147
Paignton, Devon TQ4 6YH

Printed in Torquay, Devon

Disclaimer of Liability

ACKNOWLEDGEMENTS

I would like to thank the following for their help,
enthusiasm and valuable contributions,
without whom this book would not have been possible.

John Ambler, BBC Archives Reading, Blue Water Sub Aqua Group,
British Library, Moyra Burnett, Peter Claughton, Czech Flag
Institute, David Edwards, Garter King of Arms, Greffe Office Sark,
Guernsey Evening Press, Guernsey Museums, Hampshire County
Record Office, Richard Keen, Rev. Leworthy - Vicar of Sark, Leo
Meyr, Newspaper Library Colindale, Paul A Toplis, Hugh Peskett,
Alison Robson, Public Record Office, Royal Geographical Society
London, The Company Registry - Douglas Isle of Man, The Flag
Institute, The German Occupation Museum - Guernsey, The Priaulx
Library - St Peter Port, Doctor Richard Thumerer, Geoffrey Treseder,

and many Sark Residents who prefer to remain unidentified.

With special thanks to my wife Edna for all of her help, patience and
understanding during the past two years.

Peter J Rivett

This book is dedicated to the
average Sarkese, the hewers of the
wood and the drawers of water,
who, by their unremitting toil,
enable the ruling clique to live in
the manner to which they have
become accustomed.

PREFACE

Some four years ago, I read a newspaper report that David and Frederick Barclay were claiming that their island, Brecqhou, was not part of Sark. At first, this struck me as a manifest absurdity for how could Brecqhou, situated as it is within a stone's throw of Sark, not be part of the latter?

However, I knew that the Barclay brothers were not noted for lost causes and so I started to take a more serious look at their claims. Like Saul on the road to Damascus, I have become converted to their view and my only surprise is that the matter is still unresolved.

In the course of my research, other inaccuracies about Sark and Brecqhou came to light until I had accumulated sufficient material to consider writing this book. This is not the definitive history of Sark; that has still to be written by someone far more learned than I. All that I have attempted to do is to look at what has previously been written about Sark and Brecqhou to see if it was tenable. Some of the results surprised me. I hope that you, the reader, will also be similarly affected.

Peter J Rivett
Torquay
1999

PROLOGUE

"You may take my word for it,
this place is just such another as,
to my knowledge, formerly were
the islands of Sark and Herm
between the smaller and the greater Britain.
Islands of Thieves, Banditti, Picaroons,
Robbers, Ruffians and Murtherers."

Pantagruels's Voyage
(The Fourth Book of Dr François Rabelais)

CONTENTS

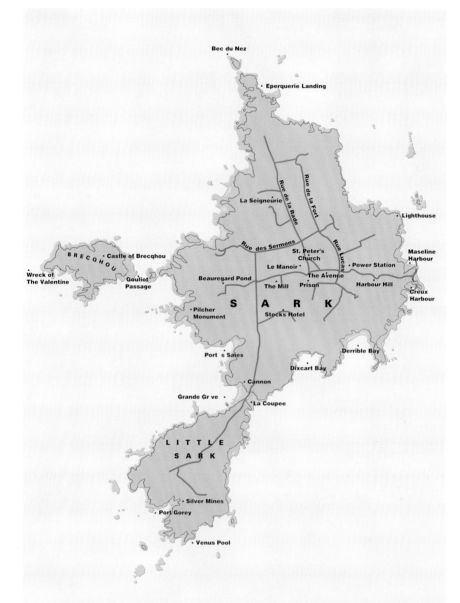

© 1999 Peter J Rivett

PART ONE

SARK

SARK
IS LIKE A HALL OF MIRRORS
WHERE NOTHING IS QUITE
WHAT IT SEEMS

CHAPTER ONE

SARK ?
BEEN THERE - GOT THE TEE-SHIRT!

Your trip to Sark invariably commences at the White Rock pier in St Peter Port, Guernsey. There you will join a vessel of the Sark Shipping Company for the 45 minute passage to your destination. The trip can range from idyllic to "quite interesting", depending upon the sea state. You will pass, quite closely in some cases, pretty fearful rocks, as well as the island of Jethou before crossing the Grand Roussel between Herm and Sark. You might even get a glimpse of the impressive castle on the island of Brecqhou, although, unless the sun is at the right angle, detail is hard to pick out. A knowledgeable fellow-traveller will tell you that it is a temple for some exotic eastern religion or a vast casino or that it has underground nuclear-proof bunkers surrounded by armed guards dressed in sinister black uniforms. Who knows ?

Rounding the northern tip of Sark at Bec du Nez you will follow the eastern coast of Sark, passing under the lighthouse at Point Robert until, with some quite tricky seamanship, you arrive at Maseline Harbour. Here, the crew who seemed only vaguely helpful in Guernsey, become intensely helpful as you are helped up the steps to the quay. Your luggage is brought up and if it is properly marked with your destination, you may forget it. It will arrive, of that have no worry. Indeed, the chances are that your luggage will be in your hotel room before you are and there are not many places in the world which can boast that standard of service.

You are required to walk a few hundred yards through a short tunnel and here you board a toast-rack conveyance pulled by a tractor. For 65p you will be whisked up the long climb of Harbour Hill in a cloud of dust. Motoring correspondents might describe the ride as "a bit stiff on the suspension" but eventually you will arrive at the Bel Air Inn where you have two choices, walk or ride in a carriage.

In the course of your stay on Sark, you will doubtless see La Coupée, that wonderful natural bridge between Big Sark and Little Sark. You may even progress further into Little Sark and see what remains of the silver mines, perhaps taking refreshments en route at La Sablonnerie Hotel.

A visit to La Seigneurie gardens is of course a "must" and there the visitor will see the cannon given by Good Queen Bess to Helier de Carteret, as well as guns taken from the very privateer commanded by Jean Allaire, a forbear of the present Seigneur.

Although Sark has no motor-cars, an ever-present hazard is the cyclist, of whom sometimes there seem to be hundreds, who silently glide up behind you. As you wander through the leafy lanes you will smell pure air, and see plants and insects long thought extinct in urban Britain. Within reason, you can wander almost anywhere on Sark, for there is no law of trespass. You may be lucky enough to join a "garden walk" where, for a modest fee, you can have a conducted tour of half a dozen superb local gardens, generally with a welcome cup of tea served at the last stop.

You will be told about the lack of taxes or divorce. You may beat your wife under certain conditions. You will be shown the prison and told the charming story about the little girl inmate who was so scared that she was allowed to serve her short sentence with the prison door left open.

In general, the food served is excellent, especially the fish. The milk is of a golden hue only older people on mainland UK would remember. Sarkese are most friendly and very appreciative that you have taken time and trouble to visit them. As there are no street lights, you will probably have brought a torch to help you through the darkness. There is little "light pollution" on Sark, so there is an opportunity to see the heavens as they were meant to be seen.

Within twenty-four hours, you will have slid into the casual routine that is Sark and after a few more days, you will view the poor day trippers as "grockles" for you are now a fully-fledged Sarkese! You will pity them the restricted time they have to see the beauties of Sark and you will be secretly glad when they go back down Harbour Hill in the evening to return to their own world, for then you will have Sark to yourself.

Alas, all good things must come to an end, and the time has come to pay your bill and set off home. A fantastic holiday and now you know all about Sark. As you turn your back on the island, you will be quite unaware of what goes on under the surface, for there is very much more to Sark than meets the eye.

OLD SARK JOKE

A very superior Englishman was travelling to Sark by boat and wishing to appear in command of the situation, remarked loudly to the Captain:
"I suppose, my man, you know where all of the rocks are?"

"No, Sir," replied the Skipper.

"Do you mean to tell me that you are in charge of this boat and yet do not know where all the rocks are?" continued the Englishman.

"That's right, Sir. I do not know where all the rocks are," retorted the Captain *"but I knows where they ain't!"*

CHAPTER TWO

THE FORMATIVE YEARS

Go back in time some 10,000 years and it would have been quite possible for an inhabitant of what is now St Malo to have walked beyond Jersey, past Sark, Brecqhou, Herm and Guernsey to dip his toes in a much narrower English Channel. The Channel Islands in those days were merely segments of a finger of land jutting out from what is now Normandy, of which the islands represented peaks of land, higher than the surrounding plain.

As the sea floor subsided and the water levels rose, the incessant wave action wore away the softer rock to gradually separate the islands from the rest of the European land mass. First Alderney and Guernsey, then Herm and Sark and finally Jersey were isolated so that by about 4,000 BC, give or take a few centuries, had it been possible to produce a map of the Channel Islands at that date, it would not have looked unfamiliar to the present-day viewer. Brecqhou probably broke away from Sark at a slightly later date and La Coupée, which links Great Sark with Little Sark, would undoubtedly have been a much wider and more substantial causeway.

The end result was Sark, an eroded plateau composed mainly of granite and granite variations and similar, geologically, to parts of Guernsey and Cornwall. The island was certainly difficult to gain access to by sea in those days; indeed, it might well have been difficult to get on to when it was landlocked. The difficulty in scaling the cliffs would have put off most would-be visitors. It may be for this reason that there are fewer remains of early man on Sark than on the more accessible Herm and Guernsey.

Some interesting minerals have been located on Sark and on Brecqhou including silver, copper, quartz, feldspar and amethystine quartz. Apart from silver, no commercial finds have been discovered and an attempt at silver mining in the 19th century was a financial disaster.

It is not known precisely when man first set foot on Sark - around 4,000 BC is a best guess. He would have been quite primitive, living by hunting and gathering edible berries and using very basic stone tools in his domestic life. Later, Guernsey certainly, if not Sark may have been visited by Phoenicians en route to the Cornish tin mines. By 150 BC, the Romans were also becoming aware of the sea routes which led from the Mediterranean to the Atlantic as they pushed westward into Gaul and then on into Brittany, finally stopping in the Channel Islands themselves. Guernsey was at the very western fringe of the Roman Empire and doubtless the invaders found the climate more acceptable than that later encountered when they crossed over to Britain. Romans would certainly have been familiar with Guernsey and the remains of a Roman ship, discovered off the harbour at St Peter Port are now being preserved.

Did the Romans actually land on Sark? It is not known. A small cache of coins and other objects dating from the Roman period were found in 1719 by William Tanquerel on land near the Manorial Mill. Declared to be "Treasure Trove" by the Sark Court and subsequently referred to as "The Sark Hoard" it was apparently sent to England on the instructions of the absentee Seigneur, Lord John Carteret. (Under Sark law, the declaration of "Treasure Trove" made the objects the property of the Seigneur). Lord John had a reputation of always being short of money so the treasure seemed to have vanished but in 1725, before it did so, the coins were identified as originating from Gaul, the inference being that they were buried by refugees from the Roman legions around 56 BC.

From about 900 AD onwards, Sark bounced around between one bishop and another. It was in the hands of the de Vernon family from about 1107 AD to 1203 AD when Sark reverted to the English Crown. In the wars between the English and French between 1203 and 1218 Sark changed hands three times, until in 1218 d'Aubigny took possession of the island as an English fief.

At that time, there was little loyalty towards the English Crown from Channel Islanders and homage by them was refused until the King acknowledged their "peculiar privileges". In 1226, Henry III confirmed "the liberties and customs belonging to them in the reigns of Henry II, Richard I and John." Royal Commissioners, in the reigns of Edward I and Edward II tried to check the rights of islanders without any progress being made. Thus, to obtain the loyalty of the Channel Islanders, we find successive monarchs all ratifying the ground given away by their predecessors.

In the Hundred Years' War, Sark was taken and re-taken by one side after another. Sark was so cruelly ravaged by the Scots, allies of the French, that it took her a long time to recover. Indeed, in 1374 Sark was described as being so destroyed as to be of no value. In 1461, France very nearly recovered a permanent foothold in the islands. In her efforts to defeat Edward IV, Margaret of Anjou arranged the cession of the great fort of Mont Orgueil in Jersey to the French but this was defeated by the local militia.

In 1499, the islands were intended to be transferred to the See of Winchester, but the Papal Bull to this effect remained unobeyed by Coutances and then was overlooked by Winchester. In 1568 the islands were finally transferred to the Bishop of Winchester.

During this period, Sark was home to none, except a few fishermen and bands of pirates, the latter pillaging France and neighbouring islands until, after a great effort, they were overcome in 1562. In 1565, as will be seen, a new chapter started for Sark.

CHAPTER THREE

THE de CARTERET DYNASTY

HELIER de CARTERET

1565-1581

The constitution of Sark, commences with the Charter of 1565, but to understand how and why that Charter came into being, we need to go back to 1563. In that year, a Royal Commission, with limited powers over the disposition of Crown lands, granted to Helier de Carteret the island of Sark, at Fee Farm, which was a type of renewable long lease. Although the actual grant has been lost, the return by the commissioners setting out the grant survives to this day at Hatfield House and reads as follows:-

> *"Here followeth souch parcelles of the queens majesties*
> *Landes in Garnsey as are letten there in fee*
> *ferme by the sayd comyssonneres in the*
> *fyft yeare of her majestyes nost Gracyous Raigne*
> *Item. more letten to Mr Helier de Carteright*
> *the Island of Sarke the old accustomed*
> *Rent therof being xvi escutes, and nowe the*
> *yerelye rent reserved ys xx escutes*
> *so that the increase of the rente ys iiii escutes"*

An escute was 2s.6d., so what the Commissioners had achieved was an increase from forty shillings to fifty shillings. They were clearly angling for a pat on the back from the Crown for achieving this increase!

In July 1565 de Carteret wrote a letter to the Privy Council petitioning that the grant be upgraded from Fee Farm to knight service in the same way that he held the Seigneurie of St Ouen in Jersey. This was a rather two-edged request, for once granted, it meant that whilst de Carteret had an obligation to defend his new possession, if he was overwhelmed by an enemy Sark came under the protection of the Crown.

In its original concept, a Fief Haubert was a full knight service. This meant that the recipient was, in theory at least, bound to supply the Crown with 40 days' military service in person. There was no full knight's service anywhere in the Channel Islands. St Ouen was the largest, at two thirds knight service and the term of the St Ouen knight's service was two thirds of forty days' service at Mount Orgueil Castle, accompanied by two armed and mounted men.

In everyday practice, however, actual physical military service became rare after the early 13th century. Those owing such service paid "scutage" or shield money instead of turning up for duty. This enabled the King to pay for professional soldiers rather than rely upon some overweight under-exercised squire turning up for forty days and then going home regardless of the tactical situation. In the case of Sark, a twentieth part of a knight's fee would have amounted to two days' service, not enough time to get anywhere near to the battlefield before the due service was completed. In any event, Channel Island knights were not bound to serve outside the islands.

Helier de Carteret's petition which exists today in Hatfield House reads as follows:

To the right honnorable the Lordes and others of the queens majesties
most honnorable privie counsell.
In his humble wise besecheth yor honnors, your daily
Oratour Helier de Carteret Sr. de sainct Owen that wheare of late
the same your saide Oratour hath taken in fee farme the Isle of Sarke with
appurtences which always sythen the expulsion of the frenche hath layen
vacaunte, as yt hath doe twoe hundreth yeres bifore their entree into
the same, Your saide Oratour waighinge and considering the inconvenience
that might happen as well as to his partycular estate,
as also the estate of all the isles nere about hath been thereby moved at
his great costis and charges to take in hand the inhabitation of the same
according to a covenent and agreement passed betwene the Queen's Majesties
late Comyssionirs in the isle of Guernesey and your honnors saide Oratour,
being Seigneur of Sainct Owen. Forasmuche therefore as your honours saide
Oratour may be the better hable to compasse that enterprise, according to the
covenant passed in that behalf yt maye please your honnors, by your good
meanses to the Quenes Majestie to gett her highnis graunt that your saide
Oratour may be have and en Joye the saide Isle of Sarke with all the
commoditis thereunto belonginge by knyghtis service in such mannir and forme
as he presently en Joyeth the Seignorie of St Owen. So, as if your saide
Oratour shall chaunce to decease (is heire beinge in none age) the saide Isle of
Sarke maye togyther with the Seignorye of St Owen be in the garde of hir
highnis for the better suretye of the same, as auncientlye the said Seignorie of
St Owen hath been accustomed in that behalf. And your saide Oratour shall
pray to almightie god for the prosperous preservation of your most honnorable
estates long to contynewe.

The petition was endorsed by Lord Cecil as follows:-

St Owen for the Ile of Sark - to be granted from the Queen's
Majesty as the Segnory of St Ouen is.

The records of the Privy Council show that de Carteret

attended on the Council on 21st July 1565 and on 6th August 1565, the Letters Patent were granted by knight service.

The Letters Patent still exist in the Public Record Office at Kew and represent a fairly standard document of its kind. Indeed it could be said to have been a standard Manorial Charter straight from a mediaeval clerk's word processor!

After the usual preamble, full of flourishes and flowery language, de Carteret was being granted, for a lump sum of £50, "all that our aforesaid island of Sark". There then follows an imposing list of the rights which accrued to him, most of which did not exist at the time of the grant! He was then required to pay, each year, one twentieth part of a knight's fee, commuted to fifty shillings (£2.50) since, as has been explained, actual knight service was both impracticable and unfashionable.

Next was a recital of revenues and profits which would accrue to de Carteret providing that within certain complex time limits, he would cause Sark to be inhabited by *"forty men at the least, being our subjects or who shall bind themselves by an oath"*. Contrary to popular myth, there was nothing in the Charter about *"Forty men with muskets"*. Muskets were not invented until around 1582. Indeed, the obligation to defend Sark is conspicuous by its absence.

The original grant of the Tenements included **nothing** about defence and it was not until about 1589 that Sark Tenement documentation included the term, *"un homme bien et suffisant pour la défence et sauvegarde de cette ditte isle..."*

De Carteret initially had some trouble in fulfilling the requirement for forty men. He offered very attractive terms such as parcels of land leased in perpetuity at low rents. A condition of such leases was that a house was to be built and that the Tenant provided a man for defence purposes, a role generally fulfilled by the Tenant himself. With de Carteret came the families, Le Cerf, Chevalier, Vibert, Le Couteur, Le Broc, Roger Guille, Le Gros, Hamon, the Alexandres and the Le Masuriers, all from Jersey.

De Carteret was no fool and one of his first deals would have been described today as "back to back leasing". He had to pay fifty shillings a year to the Crown, so he let a parcel of land, later known as Beauregard, to his friend Gosselin for fifty shillings a year as well as providing four men for defence. Thus Helier had covered his annual outgoing in one deal. Gosselin, in turn, brought the Vaudin and Du Val families with him.

Helier de Carteret reserved some 300 vergees (about 120 acres) of the prime central land for himself. Other Tenants received an allocation of land consisting of productive land and "cotils" (clifftop land useful for sheep grazing). Since each "cotil" had a piece of coastline, this was a simple method of ensuring that the entire Sark coast was supervised.

The settlement was joined by some Englishmen with particular skills, namely Smith, Dare, Brayer, Slowley and Roo. There were also some Huguenots, Jean Quesle and his wife Rémy who were, respectively, Surgeon and Midwife and of course Cosmé Brévint whose work is described in another chapter. Other members of the de Carteret family made up the forty, to be known for all time, as "the Quarantaine".

The Seigneur had the responsibility for appointing a religious adviser and in Cosmé Brévint he gained a forceful supporter of the Huguenot Reformed Church. Indeed, the concern shown by de Carteret for the pastoral care of his co-colonists contrasts markedly with the cavalier attitudes shown by later Seigneurs, especially those of the 20th century.

The task which confronted de Carteret was huge and should not be understated. One can only conjecture on the hardships which the original settlers faced, especially in winter. In 1572, we unfortunately see another departure from fact. According to popular myth, in that year de Carteret went to London where the Queen showed great interest in what he had achieved. In recognition of this, it is said, she created Sark as a Fief Haubert in its own right and gave him six cannon. This spurious event is dealt with in the next chapter. Suffice it to say that the 1572 visit and the gift of cannon were pure imagination on the part of the anonymous author of the Chroniques de Jersey in 1585.

Being a Jerseyman and as most of the other inhabitants of Sark originated from Jersey, de Carteret appointed, in 1579, Jurats and other officers with the overall aim of having an independent Sark Court based upon the Jersey model. For a while, Guernsey seemed to have ignored this development.

However, in September 1581, the Royal Court of Guernsey summoned de Carteret to explain by what authority he had acted in the way that he had. De Carteret, as was his custom, ignored the summons but unfortunately died in the same year.

Thus ended the reign of Sark's first Seigneur, undoubtedly a bold pioneer and one who laid a firm foundation for others to build upon.

CHAPTER FOUR

"THIS ROYAL THRONE OF KINGS, THIS SCEPTER'D ISLE"

William Shakespeare
Richard II
Act (ii) Sc (i)

Whilst Helier de Carteret's name is honoured in Sark for being responsible for the recolonisation of the island, there is another claim to fame which, as far as the author is aware, has never been given the prominence it deserves.

Helier de Carteret is directly related to HRH Prince William, eventual heir to the British Throne. The family tree linking Helier de Carteret with Lord John Carteret is familiar to anyone reading Ewan and de Carteret's "The Fief of Sark" so it is not proposed to repeat it here. The full family tree is very complex and what follows is an abbreviated but direct line picking up where Ewan and de Carteret's book leaves off.

Lord John Carteret married **Frances Worsley.**
One of their daughters,
Lady Georgiana Caroline Carteret married **John Spencer.**
Their son,
John, the 1st Earl Spencer, married **Margaret Georgiana Poyntz.**
Their son,

George, the 2nd Earl Spencer, married **Lady Lavinia Bingham.**
Their son,
John Charles, the 3rd Earl Spencer married **Esther Acklom.**
They had no children so the title went to younger brother **Frederick.**
Frederick, the 4th Earl Spencer, married
Elizabeth Georgiana Poyntz.
(His first wife, he married again, see below.)
Their son,
John Poyntz Spencer, the 5th Earl Spencer, married
Charlotte Frances Frederiks Seymour.
They had no children.
The title therefore went to his half-brother **Charles Robert Spencer,**
son of the 5th Earl's second wife
Adelaide Horatia Elizabeth Seymour.
Charles Robert Spencer, the 6th Earl Spencer, married
Margaret Baring.
Their son,
Albert Edward John Spencer, the 7th Earl Spencer, married **Lady
Cynthia Elinor Beatrix Hamilton.**
Their son,
Edward John Spencer, The 8th Earl Spencer,
(and Viscount Althorp)
married the **Hon Frances Ruth Burke Roache.**
Their daughter,
Diana Frances Spencer, married HRH **Prince Charles.**
Their sons, **Prince William** and **Prince Harry** are heirs in line to
the Crown of the United Kingdom.

It does not end there for there is also a direct connection between Lord John Carteret and the Duchess of York. The starting point is again Lord John's marriage.

Lord John Carteret married **Frances Worsley.**

Their other daughter,
Lady Louisa Carteret married Thomas Thynne
(2nd Viscount Weymouth).
Their son,
Thomas Thynne (2nd Marquess of Bath) married
Lady Isabella Elizabeth Byng.
Their daughter,
Lady Charlotte Anne Thynne married
Walter Francis Montague-Douglas-Scott,
(7th Duke of Queensbury).
Their son,
William Henry Walton Montague-Douglas-Scott married
Lady Louisa Jane Hamilton.
Their son,
Herbert Andrew Montague-Douglas-Scott married
Maria Josephine Agnes Edwards.
Their daughter,
Marian Louisa Montague-Douglas-Scott married
Andrew Henry Ferguson.
Their Son,
Ronald Ivor Ferguson married Susan Wright.
Their younger daughter is
Sarah Margaret Ferguson, Duchess of York.

One is tempted to add in the terms of a well-known TV game show, "Didn't they do well?" Can we look forward to Sark's first Blue Plaque being put up at Le Manoir?

CHAPTER FIVE

THE de CARTERET DYNASTY

THE GREAT MYTH OF 1572

In 1585, an anonymous manuscript entitled, "The Chroniques de Jersey" first saw the light of day. Whilst it was subsequently known to only a few scholars, it was never really considered in depth until 1832, when a rather poor translation was published by George S Syvret. In 1858, a more scholarly translation was published by A Mourant.

Although the title might imply a history of the island of Jersey, the manuscript is more of a series of accolades to the de Carteret family, so much so that independent historians have described the Chroniques as having been written by a "propagandiste des Carterets". Indeed, the Chroniques actually end with a glorification of the marriage of Philippe de Carteret, Helier's eldest son and heir. Furthermore, the published edition carries the following telling observation:

> "*Le Chroniqueur a une prédilection marquée pour les De Carteret, il nous le peint sous les couleurs les plus avantageuses: d'aprés lui, ils ont toutes les qualités toutes les vertus etc. etc.*"

The Chroniques refer to a journey that Helier de Carteret made

29

to England to meet the Queen and to show her and the Privy Council the progress that had been made with Sark. He is said to have produced a map showing Sark. As a mark of her gratitude, so the story goes, the Queen gave Helier de Carteret a new Charter dated the 25th year of her reign 1572 and a gift of guns, being 2 Demi-Culverins, 2 Sakers and 2 Falcons, together with shot, powder and the normal appurtenances for such pieces of artillery. She also invested Helier de Carteret with Sark as a Fief Haubert for one twentieth part of a knight's fee.

Whilst the question of the guns is dealt with elsewhere, the fact is that de Carteret **already held Sark as a Fief Haubert,** as has been clearly demonstrated in the preceding chapter. There is no evidence that de Carteret appeared before the Queen in 1572. Indeed, it would have been very impolite and considerably unwise to ask Her Majesty for something she had already granted some seven years earlier!

A point which is debatable is whether in fact Sark was ever a Fief Haubert anyway. There is a body of opinion which states that only a full fief can be haubert and there were none of these in the Channel Islands.

A glaring error in the Chroniques is that 1572 was not the 25th year of the reign of Queen Elizabeth. The 25th regnal year would have spanned from 17th November 1582 to 16th November 1583. Helier de Carteret died in 1581.

It would seem that the Chronicler confused the dates of three events. These were, 1565 when Helier de Carteret did in fact see the Privy Council in connection with his petition, 1572 when he was in correspondence with the Privy Council (but not present in person), regarding procedures for appeals from the Royal Court of Jersey and 1582 when Philippe de Carteret went to London to do homage to her Majesty upon inheriting the Fiefs of Jersey and Sark upon the death of his father, Helier de Carteret.

Helier de Carteret was a God-fearing man and a committed member of the church. So much so, that on each occasion he visited

London, he made it his business to attend the French Church in what is now Threadneedle Street. The records of attendance of the French Church still exist and in 1561, the entry reads, in the original style of writing:

"Le dyt jour 3 dapril anno 1561, se presentirent a nostre Consistoire ung gentilhomme de lisle de garnisey nomme helier de Carteret."

and for 29th March 1565:

"Joeudy se presenty ung gentil homme de gernesey nomme de Carteret".

For the year 1572, there is no entry whatsoever. Given that a visit to London often spanned many months it is unlikely that a person of de Carteret's strong religious beliefs would not have "popped into church" had he been in London that year.

In 1607, a Royal Commissioner visited Jersey, Sark and Guernsey preparing an extente (survey) of Crown revenues and examining Crown rights, etc. They reported that Philippe de Carteret held Sark, "by Letters Patent under the Broad (Great) Seale of England dated vi. to die Augusti Anno R.Regine nuper Elizabeth the viii.mo" i.e. 6th August 1565.

De Carteret must have actually had to exhibit his Charter to the Commissioners who quoted the Latin date. If at that time, de Carteret had a better Charter granted in 1572, as the Chroniques allege, he surely would have produced it to the Commissioners in 1607. He did not do so because, quite simply, it did not exist. Indeed, in March 1921, in response to a question from the Lieutenant Governor of Guernsey, the Home Office in London reported that they had been assured by the Public Record Office that there was no later Charter than the one of 1565.

Accepting that the Chronicler confused three separate events, the question has to be asked how subsequent historians of Sark did not wonder how it was possible for de Carteret to be granted Sark as a Fief Haubert in 1565 and again in 1572. One proposition is that in 1565, Helier de Carteret was "Seigneur of St Ouen" **and** "Seigneur of Sark". Thereafter the normal contraction of written and spoken language described him as "Seigneur of St Ouen and Sark" until it appeared that he had one Seigneurie covering part of Jersey and the island of Sark. This seems to explain why subsequent historians refer to the 1565 Charter as "granting Sark as an adjunct to St Ouen" and the non-existent 1572 Charter as "splitting Sark from St Ouen."

Regrettably, it is all fiction. There was never any event in 1572 remotely like that described by the Chroniques de Jersey and repeated by historians ever since.

CHAPTER SIX

THE CURIOUS CASE
OF THE SEIGNEUR'S GUN

The cannon depicted above is to be found in the gardens of La Seigneurie, home of the present Seigneur. Without doubt, it is a very interesting cannon and has, it is said, an unusual claim to fame. The story goes that in 1572, Helier de Carteret, the first Seigneur, went to London and Queen Elizabeth was so pleased at what he had done with Sark, she presented him with six cannon together with powder, shot and other accoutrements as a token of her esteem. Furthermore, she had engraved on at least one of the cannon, the following inscription:

Don de Sa Majesté La Royne Elizabeth
au Seigneur de Sercq
A.D. 1572

To prove the event, there, in the grounds of La Seigneurie is a bronze cannon with such an inscription. Truly a remarkable story - unfortunately, also a completely false one.

The first reference to these guns is contained in the Chroniques de Jersey, written around 1585 and known to scholars from that time but not published until 1832.

According to the Chroniques, Helier de Carteret went to London in 1572 and after explaining to the Queen what he had achieved in Sark, she gave him a new Charter dated the 25th year of her reign and the year 1572. The Chroniques list the guns in some detail, there being 2 Demi-Culverins weighing 29 hundredweight each, 2 Sakers, each weighing 16 hundredweight and 2 Falcons of 9 hundredweight each.

The first error of fact is that there was never a "new charter of 1572". Sark was founded by the Charter of 1565, a fact admitted by every historian. There is no trace of a charter dated 1572 in any record depository, nor of any cross reference in any other relevant documents. Every subsequent document of importance refers back in its narrative to the 1565 Letters Patent. 1572 appears only in storybooks.

The second error of fact is that the 25th year of Elizabeth's reign would have run from 17th November 1582 to 16th November 1583 by which date Helier de Carteret was deceased.

The third error of fact is that no guns were issued in 1572 to Sark. In those days, guns were kept in the Tower of London and only released upon presentation of a warrant from the Privy Council. No guns were issued to either Sark or de Carteret in that year. The records survive to this day.

34

The fourth error of fact is that guns were far too valuable to be given out willynilly as gifts. They were sent to where the strategic need was perceived and brought back again when the danger had passed. Indeed, the local practice was that the Crown supplied, but retained ownership of, the cannon, whilst the local inhabitants were expected to provide a site for their installation and to pay the wages of the gunners.

In 1593, there were indeed cannon on Sark which the then Seigneur freely acknowledged to be the property of the Crown. These were four each of Demi-Culverins, Falcons and Sakers. The Seigneur wrote to the authorities in London requesting powder and shot for these weapons plus new carriages. From this, it is possible to deduce that these cannon might have been supplied circa 1583 when there was a lot of fortification work going on in the Channel Islands in connection with the wars with Spain. This date also ties in with the 25th year of the reign of Good Queen Bess. By 1593, given the use of unseasoned wood, rough treatment and ten years of exposure to Sark elements, it is entirely rational that the new gun carriages would be required. There was, in that year, a renewed threat from Spain; indeed in 1595, Spanish soldiers landed at Penzance and burned the town.

At this point, it is not unreasonable to ask about the cannon in the Seigneurie gardens. It is certainly bronze, almost certainly English, and could just date from the late 16th century. However, it is far too small to be one of the guns previously mentioned. With a calibre of 1.5 inches, at best it would project a cannon ball weighing 12 ounces, some 100 yards. In terms of size and calibre, it resembles a "Robinet"- hardly likely to deter the Spanish fleet! Then there is the inscription which contains a number of fundamental errors.

Firstly, the use of La Royne, instead of La Reyne, points to the use of contemporary Guernsey French rather than classical French.

Secondly, Helier de Carteret was *"Seigneur de St Ouen et de Sercq"*. It is inconceivable that he would have used a lesser title especially when his Jersey interests were far more important than those of Sark. The Seigneur of St Ouen was the senior Seigneur in the entire Channel

Islands. People of that era were very touchy about being addressed by an incorrect title and for Helier de Carteret to have been addressed solely as "Seigneur de Sercq" would have been quite insulting on either side of the English Channel. The de Carterets always used the "two fief" title, for example, in the 1681 litigation the then Seigneur was designated, *"Baronet Seigneur de St Ouen, Serc & etc."* In St Peter's church on Sark a tablet placed in 1885 to commemorate Helier de Carteret shows the 'two-fief' title.

Thirdly, in 1572, the possessive pronoun was used with a lower case letter in both English and French, thus Sa Majesté should have been sa Majesté. This was the position for many years after 1572, certainly until the mid to late 18th century.

Fourthly, it is highly unlikely that in 1572 the date would have been inscribed as A.D. 1572, but would have been expressed in Roman form and written "l'an mil v.c.lxxii" or some variant thereon.

Fifthly, when a photograph transparency of the inscription is magnified, there is a hint, to put it no higher, that the "5" in 1572 started life as a "6" which would indicate that the inscription was put on at a later date. It is reasonable to assume that no person commencing to inscribe the figures 1572 in the year 1572 would be likely to start inscribing 1672 in error, whereas someone carving the inscription at a later date might just make such an error in a moment of inattention.

Finally, the calligraphy used is crude and certainly not of a standard which might be expected if the work had been performed in London at the express command of Her Majesty.

The first time the title would quite properly have been solely **"Seigneur de Sercq"** would have been after 1721 when the ownership of Sark passed out of the de Carteret family. The only logical conclusion that can be drawn is that the Seigneurie cannon is a hoax. Had the cannon been lying around on Sark prior to this period, it is felt that the Parliamentarians, who sequestrated and occupied Sark during the English Civil War, would have melted it down. Cromwell's men were very fond of melting down metals, as is evidenced by the many churches in England which lost their lead roofs.

Failing that, one of the Le Pelleys might have been tempted to sell it to finance the silver mines; a bronze gun, even one of such modest proportions, would have had quite a value which could have been converted into cash.

The best hypothesis to date is that the inscription was carried out sometime between 1852 and 1859 at the behest of the Reverend William T Collings (the Seigneur). The actual inscription is not recorded in the Chroniques de Jersey so any written references to the inscribed gun could only have arisen after the date on which the inscription was executed.

Guide books and accounts of visits to Sark before 1845, some by relatives of the Le Pelleys, carry no mention of an inscribed cannon at the Seigneurie. For example, in 1835, H D Inglis was escorted around Sark by Seigneur Le Pelley and entertained by him at the Seigneurie. The object was to gather material for a book to be written by Inglis called "The Channel Islands". It would have been inconceivable for the Seigneur not to have shown off the inscribed cannon to his important guest, had it existed then. There was, however, a bronze gun at the Seigneurie in 1852 but it is not recorded as having been inscribed at that date.

The first mention of an inscribed cannon found by the author is in 1859 when a book was published called, "Handbook to the Island of Sark". Since the Le Pelleys were far too busy in the 1840's trying to keep the Seigneurial ship afloat, the "culprit" must be the first Seigneur Collings. It is highly significant that a more erudite version of the Chroniques de Jersey became available in 1858.

It is not thought for one moment that this worthy reverend gentleman wished to mislead or falsify history. The Seigneur was a military enthusiast. He would probably have recently read the published version of the Chroniques de Jersey, taken them at face value and decided to inscribe the cannon he found in the Seigneurie grounds

37

to embellish a good yarn.

Where the gun might have come from is open to speculation. One possible source is that it could have been salvaged from the East Indiaman *Valentine* in 1776. It is however difficult but not impossible to envisage such a vessel carrying an Elizabethan gun.

There are, cut along the centre-line of the gun, three "sighting" marks which, by their precision, could point to the piece having been operationally used after the Elizabethan era. It might have been a private possession of the captain of the *Valentine*, or possibly simply used as a saluting gun. Contemporary writers who dealt with the stranding of the *Valentine* state that two cannon were salvaged by the Seigneur. One was pressed into service by the Sark militia, being a more modern piece. The other one may well be the gun which sits today in the Seigneurie gardens. Interestingly enough, its existence was considered worth recording in the Contract of Sale of the Fief of Sark in 1852 between Pierre Le Pelley and Marie Allaire.

The best hypothesis is that it was recovered from the *Valentine* by Le Pelley and was later inscribed by the first Seigneur Collings. Wherever the Seigneurie cannon actually came from however, one thing is absolutely certain, it did not come from the Tower of London in 1572 and it was certainly not presented by Queen Elizabeth I.

CHAPTER SEVEN

THE de CARTERET DYNASTY

PHILIPPE de CARTERET
1581 -1594

In May 1582, the Procureur of Guernsey submitted to the Court that Sark was part and parcel of the island of Guernsey and that the jurisdiction of a Bailiff and Jurats for Sark was not legal. Shortly afterwards, the Bailiff of Guernsey went to Sark to see for himself. A little later, the Royal Court found the Bailiff of Sark to be a usurper without authority and promptly clapped him into prison.

Clearly the Guernsey Authorities were out for blood for they followed up this victory by seeking and obtaining "possession et saisine". As heir to Helier de Carteret, Philippe was required to pay a sum of money called "première saisine" to his feudal overlord upon succeeding to the Fief. Philippe refused to pay.

In 1582 Philippe de Carteret as heir to Helier, went to England to do homage to the Queen for his lands in Jersey and Sark. In March 1582, Sir Thomas Leighton, Governor of Guernsey, wrote to Cecil to warn him that Philippe was on his way and Cecil minuted that de Carteret was not to be admitted to do homage until the issues of the Sark constitution were resolved. The Privy Council wrote to Governor Leighton in June 1582 that de Carteret had arrived in London and they sought the views of Governor Leighton on the Sark problem. Correspondence continued and Secretary Walsingham became involved in 1583. On 24th April 1583 the definitive Order in Council was drawn up and on 20th May of that year, de Carteret, then back in Jersey, wrote to Walsingham thanking him for his good offices.

Thus the dispute was settled. Sark got its Court, Philippe got his Fief back upon payment of £40 as première saisine. This settlement, which could be described as a defining moment in the history of Sark, gathered up a number of points and codified these into law. The major points are as follows:-

Military matters appertain to the Captain in Guernsey.
Civil jurisdiction could be dealt with by five Sark Jurats.
A Clerk to the Court be appointed by the Seigneur.
A Prévot to be appointed by the Seigneur.
A Constable and Vingtenier to be appointed by the inhabitants.
Ecclesiastical matters to be under the Bishop of Winchester.
The Seigneur is not bound to serve in Chief Pleas of Guernsey.
Wrecks of the sea appertain to the Seigneur.
Treizième and Firmage appertain to the Seigneur.
Conger House (Esperquerie des Congres) not to apply in Sark.
Weights and measures as for Guernsey.
Sarkese to observe the ancient customs.
Sark not to be subject to Guernsey ordinance re. grain etc.
Chief Pleas should meet three times a year.

Although a Sark Court was approved by the 1583 Order in Council this did not materialise until 1594 after Philippe's death. However, work on the tunnel to Creux Harbour was completed in 1588, giving the island's fishermen access to some limited shelter from the sea. In 1585, he was instrumental in making a new ordinance regarding the upkeep of the roads, which henceforth was to fall upon the shoulders of Tenants.

Around 1580, several of the original colonists had died, and the question of inheritance arose for the first time. In Jersey, the eldest son got the house and the fowl run, the widow was protected by her "dower" and the remainder of the property was divided amongst the other heirs. Since some of these resided outside Sark and had no particular interest in moving to Sark, they endeavoured to sell these parcels of land to others. Thus fragmentation of the original Forty Tenements commenced and this alarmed Philippe de Carteret. His view was that not only was his rent roll threatened, but a Tenement might be so divided as to no longer support a man and thus might impair his ability to defend the island when required.

Philippe tried to stem this practice in 1593 and whilst he was successful to some degree, he could not upset those sub-divisions that had already been registered. Matters were made worse by Nicholas Guille trying to sub-divide the Tenement of Dosdane into three parts. To cap it all, Philippe died in 1594 before any corrective action could be taken.

CHAPTER EIGHT

THE de CARTERET DYNASTY

PHILIPPE de CARTERET
1594-1643

Philippe de Carteret was ten years of age when he succeeded to the Seigneurie of Sark, and as a consequence of his minority, his uncle, Amice de Carteret, a Jurat of the Jersey Court, acted as Seigneur. One of his first moves was to formally set up the Sark Court, created by the Order in Council of 1583, but which, like many things on Sark, "was a long time a'coming".

Amice was later appointed Bailiff of Guernsey and so had to relinquish his Office in Jersey. It was because of this that Sark tended to veer more towards Guernsey than had earlier been the case. In 1605, young Philippe came of age and took up the reins.

Also in that year it was decided by Chief Pleas that in future only successors in title to the original Forty Tenements could sit and vote in Chief Pleas. These became known as Les Maisons de la Quarantaine to differentiate them from the Tenants who owned land but had no defence obligations. Young Philippe's mind was still exercised by the question of succession and the possibility that with the sub-division of Tenements and the growing practice of raising cash by mortgage on them, his defence strategy might be undermined.

He thus applied to the Crown and was given a further grant called the Letters Patent of 1611. This clearly set out that land was to pass to the eldest son and that furthermore land was indivisible and could not be pledged to raise a mortgage.

In 1612, Philippe started to issue revised contracts to certain newly-inherited Tenants incorporating the requirements of the Letters Patent. This date is also the earliest mention of the word "musket" which appears in a contract for La Colinette, which actually uses the phrase:-

....*Fourny d'un mousket ses provisions et appurtenances"*...

From about that date, Philippe seems to have switched his energies to Jersey in an effort to re-establish the high position held by the family and in 1616 he received a knighthood.

Inertia, being the most powerful driving force on Sark, meant that the Letters Patent of 1611 were not promptly registered in the Sark Court and there were further divisions of landed estate. By now Sir Philippe had become both Bailiff and Lieutenant Governor of Jersey and Sark was far from his mind. In London, the schism between Monarch and Parliament had widened into the Civil War and it is an opportune point to break away from Sark to study briefly the effect of the English Civil War on the Channel Islands.

In 1642, the division between King Charles and Parliament erupted into open warfare and the English Civil War commenced. Jersey favoured the King, Guernsey favoured Parliament. Sark was "piggy in the middle" and was aligned with Guernsey. A faction within Royalist Jersey, for their own personal reasons, decided to support the Parliamentary cause and forced Philippe de Carteret into Elizabeth Castle where he was besieged for several months. Parliament, upon hearing of this, deprived de Carteret of the Fiefs of St Ouen and Sark and confiscated all of the revenues arising therefrom.

In August 1643, a bout of sickness broke out in Elizabeth Castle and Philippe de Carteret died. His son, also rather unimaginatively called Philippe, continued to fight.

CHAPTER NINE

THE de CARTERET DYNASTY

PHILIPPE de CARTERET

1643-1662

In November 1643, the siege of Elizabeth Castle was lifted by the arrival of a force commanded by George Carteret, an English Naval Captain who was a cousin of Philippe de Carteret but who had shortened his name because he felt that its French sound would not advance his career in the Royal Navy. By 1644, the cousins had formulated plans to re-take Sark for the King. In 1645 the attack was launched, but failed abysmally. Whilst neither the Quarantaine nor the garrison stopped the invasion, the intervention of the Parliamentary frigate out of Guernsey eventually repulsed the invading force.

In April 1646, Prince Charles, the King's son, was sent to Jersey and in the same year knighted Philippe de Carteret for services to the royalist cause. In 1648 yet another attempt was made to capture Sark, but this was thwarted by exceptionally bad weather. With the execution of King Charles I his heir Prince Charles was proclaimed King in Jersey.

The Restoration of the Monarchy in May 1660 rebounded to the advantage of the de Carterets who have been described as one of the few Royalist families who ended the Civil War better off financially than when it started. In August 1660, the Fief of Sark was formally restored to Sir Philippe de Carteret but his reign was to be short-lived for he died in February 1662 to be succeeded by his son, a minor aged eleven. It is a sad fact that the de Carteret line seemed to have very little imagination over Christian names so that in 1662, yet another Seigneur called Philippe took over the helm of Sark.

CHAPTER TEN

THE de CARTERET DYNASTY

PHILIPPE de CARTERET
1662-1693

Because Philippe was only eleven years old when he succeeded to the Fief, the authority of the Seigneur was exercised by Nicholas Richardson on behalf of Anne Dumaresq, the widow of the previous Seigneur. This enabled the Le Gros family, ably assisted by Elie Brévint, the Minister, to exercise considerable personal control over the island. More land transactions were executed in contravention of the Letters Patent of 1611.

When Philippe attained his majority, he set about correcting some wrongs of the past. This was not easy because the main offenders were the Le Gros family who had a stranglehold on the Sark Court. By using his powerful family connections with the English Court he sought and obtained an Order in Council suspending the Sark Court in the form in which it then existed and substituting a new Court with a different structure. Under the new hierarchy the Court would be made up of the Seneschal, the Prévot and the Greffier, all to be appointed by the Seigneur without any need to consult with the Tenants. This arrangement is the one which exists today.

His next step was to seek an order from the Royal Court in Guernsey that the infringements of the 1611 Letters Patent were unlawful and should be rectified. In the course of time, the Guernsey Jurats agreed that his complaints were justified and those parties who had dismembered Tenements had a year and a day to rectify the matter. Some Tenants did actually undo previous conveyances, but in the main it was found to be impracticable to try to restore the Sark Tenements to the form in which they existed in 1565. In the end, and after a protracted struggle, a compromise was reached.

Thereafter Philippe appears to have lost interest in Sark. He became Bailiff of Jersey in 1682 but then became closely involved with events taking place at the Court in London. This was at the time of the accession of a Catholic king and this time, the de Carterets bet on the wrong horse by supporting King James. When the latter was defeated at the Battle of the Boyne, Philippe was left in some financial disarray. He leased out the rights of being Seigneur to one Daniel Valpy for three years in exchange for a capital sum, but before this agreement had run its course Philippe died in 1693.

CHAPTER ELEVEN

THE de CARTERET DYNASTY

SIR CHARLES de CARTERET and LORD JOHN CARTERET

1693-1720

Sir Charles had the distinction of being raised to knight status at the age of eight. At the age of fifteen he became Seigneur of St Ouen and Sark which estates were so financially drained as to be a millstone around his neck. His Tenants in Jersey later saw this as an opportunity to revolt against the performance of feudal services. He counter attacked by seizing their Tenements. Complaints were made that Sir Charles was totally unsuited to his hereditary post of Bailiff of Jersey because he barely spoke French and spent too much time in London where he was a Gentleman of the Privy Chamber. In trying to keep up with the champagne tastes of London, with the beer money arising from St Ouen and Sark he eventually sought, and was granted, permission to sell both fiefs.

However, before he could do this he died in 1715; thus was extinguished the senior branch of the de Carteret family. The fiefs passed to Lord John Carteret, the son of Lord George Carteret whose grandfather was the chap who changed his name slightly to avoid compromising his naval career.

As far as is known, Lord John never visited the Channel Islands and whilst he made some effort to lift the debt of his Estates, he eventually used the Royal permission given to Sir Charles to sell the Fief of Sark.

Although technically Seigneur from 1715 to 1720, it would, in view of his non-attendance in Sark, be wrong to place him in the same category as those de Carterets who, for good or ill, had diligently attended to their duties as Seigneur.

CHAPTER TWELVE

THE SEIGNEUR WHO NEVER WAS!

COLONEL JOHN JOHNSON

Legend has it that on the 3rd September 1720, Lord John Carteret sold the Fief of Sark to an Englishman, Colonel Johnson, who was once in command of the garrison in Guernsey and who had advanced a lot of money to Sir Charles de Carteret. Legend also has it that the agent arranging the deal ran off with the money so that Lord John received none of the proceeds. If a mortgage was granted in favour of Colonel Johnson it was invalid because it carried no Crown permission to alienate. Possibly the English form of mortgage was used, i.e. a conveyance with a right of redemption, which some mistake as a pure conveyance.

The sequence of events can be summarised as follows:-

Sir Charles de Carteret had Crown Licence by letters Patent of 1713 to bequeath Sark etc. to trustees appointed by his will.

In due course, Sir Charles appointed trustees under a will.

In 1715, Sir Charles died.

In 1720, a private Act of Parliament appointed new trustees to whom the licence to alienate was undoubtedly transferred. It is possible that this Act was introduced to thwart any claim Colonel Johnson might have had on Sark, but this is mere speculation.

In 1721, those new trustees conveyed the Fief of Sark to James Milner of which more anon.

From this it will be seen that there is no mention of Colonel Johnson, nor any "time window" for him to have become involved. The best guess is that Sir Charles did in fact execute a mortgage, which a Court would have held to be ultra vires. Doubtless, being a man desperately short of money, he had it registered at the Sark Greffe to give it the appearance of legitimacy. Historians have inspected the records at the Greffe Office and have probably confused the documentation there with a legal alienation of the Fief. It may be that Sir Charles's request for a Licence to Alienate in 1714 was an attempt to put right the previous illegality.

However, Colonel Johnson was never a Seigneur of Sark.

CHAPTER THIRTEEN

MORE LIKE CARETAKERS THAN SEIGNEURS

JAMES MILNER and
THE BISHOP OF GLOUCESTER
1721-1730

James Milner was a trader operating between Portugal and London. He purchased Sark by Deed of Bargain and Sale, in the English legal form on 30th August 1721 from the trustees appointed by the Act of Parliament of 1720. On 29th September 1721 he made a Will appointing Joseph Wilcocks, then a prebendary of Westminister but later to become the Bishop of Gloucester, as his executor and trustee.

Milner and his brother had a reputation of sorts in the Portuguese trade and Wilcocks had, at one time, been an Anglican chaplain in Lisbon, so that may well have been how they became acquainted. Milner died on 24th November 1721 and on 4th January 1722, Joseph, Bishop of Gloucester was granted probate.

The Will, after taking into account certain specific pecuniary legacies, left his entire residuary estate which consisted of lands in Yorkshire and Lincolnshire (specifically named) and Sark (not named) to his four nieces. Three of the nieces were unmarried; the fourth was married to the Bishop of Gloucester.

Sark was a Feudal Estate, held of the Crown as to a twentieth part of a knight's fee and not devisable by will. Under English Feudal Law, the four nieces would have inherited as co-heiresses. However, although the Feudal Tenure Act of 1660 abolished feudal tenure in England, Sark, having its feudal roots in the English system, the rules applicable to feudal tenures before 1660 would still have applied. After all, in spite of Sark's predilection for things Norman, Sark as far as the documentation went, was an English manor.

It is debatable, when the succession of the Fief of Sark opens to female heirs, whether the eldest sister succeeds as sole heiress or all of the sisters succeed as joint heiresses. There is a strong argument that in 1927, both of the Collings's daughters should have succeeded to the Seigneurie, rather than Dame Sibyl alone.

In 1730, when the youngest of the girls had come of age, the Bishop of Gloucester sought, and was granted as trustee, licence to alienate Sark and this he did to Susan le Gros, otherwise known as Le Pelley.

To square the circle, there were two conveyances involved, one from the Bishop to Susan Le Pelley and one from each of the four co-heiresses to Susan Le Pelley.

Thus started the next Seigneurial dynasty, that of the Le Pelley family.

OLD SARK

"On Good Friday and Easter Monday we go up to the pond at Beauregard and sail toy boats. I don't think anyone knows why we do it, for no one, not even children, sail toy boats on any other days. It is just an old custom."

"We have a prison, but it's only been used twice in a hundred years. A girl was put there for stealing some clothes, but she was frightened of being shut up, so the door was left open so that her friends could talk to her."

"During the long winter evenings in Sark we make our own amusements. There are no cinemas or theatres. We have a silent film now and again at the Recreation Hall and that is the only time most of us have seen a train. We get the idea that trains spend a lot of their time just missing motor-cars at level crossings."

"The great events on Sark were Les Veilles, the Watches, when to save light and fires people gathered at one another's houses in turn, to knit and talk and play games, which often developed into a good party."

"We have a very good custom for New Year's Day. Everybody has a gun on Sark and we all take our guns and shoot. We shoot anywhere, anytime, at birds, rabbits, trees, hedges, gates - anything at all. Of course some people also get shot but we have not killed anyone yet. I don't know how old the custom is but anyway it's a good way to finish one year and start another."

"Over in the corner is the 'jonquière', the green bed, which is always to be seen in the kitchen of a Sark house. The corner is boxed in to make a large bed, then boarded over and covered in green baize. Under the bed, i.e. in the box, the furze is stored all ready chopped for the fire. When men come in from the fields, or after a meal, they lie on the bed and rest, a hard bed for hard people. If anyone comes in with news or gossip they sit on the green bed and we all gather round. There are no newspapers in Sark but the green bed does not miss much of the local news."

CHAPTER FOURTEEN

THE DAY THE EARTH MOVED

The date was 22nd December 1843. The weather was remarkably mild and still and had been since the middle of the month with light winds veering between south and east. About four o'clock in the afternoon, the whole island of Sark was alarmed by a very peculiar sound, some said like thunder. Others likened it to the passage of a heavy railway train over stone sleepers as the noise and jar increases perceptibly on its approach.

At its height, there was a rustling sound and commotion in the air, like a large bird beating its wings in a confined space. The house shook and appeared to reel as if elevated by a wave passing underneath it. This was immediately followed by a jerk, which threw some persons down and caused glasses and fire-irons to jar and some large stones to become dislodged from walls and chimneys.

The duration of sound and agitation must have been eight to ten seconds as persons were able to exchange a few words during its continuance and the immediate impulse was to rush out of the house. Oddly, no shock was felt in the silver mines, although the steam engine almost stopped and other machinery became agitated.

On 12th February 1844, another milder shock was felt and as the Wesleyan Chapel was sitting, the event was made the subject of a very profound evening discourse! The end of the world is nigh, perhaps? This second shock was also felt in Guernsey and in Devon.

In February 1929, Sark, together with the rest of the Channel Islands, was treated to a display of frost and snow which happens, hopefully, only once in a lifetime. There were snowdrifts and 13 degrees of frost in St Peter Port. Enormous icicles, more like stalactites, hung down from the Sark harbour tunnel and Harbour Hill was completely impassable to horses. Thirty volunteers took on the task of carrying mail, coal and other merchandise up from the harbour to the top of the island. To reduce bulk goods to manageable proportions, bread was put into small sacks, oil was transferred into retail measures and the large sides of meat were treated to the butcher's art on the quayside rather than in the shops.

CHAPTER FIFTEEN

THE LAST VOYAGE OF THE *VALENTINE*

The *Valentine* was an armed merchant vessel of 690 tons belonging to the Honourable East India Company. Built by Perry's at their great shipyard at Blackwall and launched in 1767, it was a three-decker, 135 ft in length and some 34 ft in width. For its first two voyages to China, it was under the command of Captain Charles Purvis but command changed in 1772 to Captain James Ogilvie when it completed another voyage to China. In 1776, it embarked on its fourth and final voyage, this time to India and back.

East India Company vessels were purpose built for the job and were generally run for four voyages, after which they were replaced. The Captain of an East Indiaman had, in addition to his pay, the right of free outward freight totalling 50 tons and free return freight rights amounting to 20 tons. Thus each Captain stood to make from £4,000 to £5,000 per voyage from skilful utilisation of this free cargo space and obviously had a financial as well as a professional interest in making a safe passage.

The ship's log of this vessel survives and although Captain Ogilvie, as a Scot, was not given to wasting words, there were occasions on the voyage when he was forced to expand beyond mere comments about the weather. On 15th October 1776, with *Valentine* safely out of dry dock, Captain Ogilvie came on board at Gravesend. After fitting out and loading with cargo for the East, *Valentine* finally departed from

The Nore, in company with the East India Company's yacht on 23rd December 1776, arriving at Portsmouth on Christmas Day.

On New Year's Day 1777 *Valentine*, in company with another Indiaman, *Egmount*, departed for Madeira arriving there on 18th January. It left Funchal on 3rd February en route for The Cape of Good Hope. Captain Ogilvie noted in the log on 4th April, *"Punished Charles Graham, 12 lashes for fighting and making a disturbance"*. On 4th April, *Valentine* met up with *Resolution* and *Worcester*, also Indiamen. Captain Ogilvie was obviously the junior for he sent his boat to *Resolution* for instructions from Captain Pointon. On 17th April they arrived at the Cape but did not stay long, departing on 24th April.

On 24th May whilst in the Indian Ocean, Captain Ogilvie *"exercised the great guns and small arms"*. The exact armament carried by *Valentine* has not been ascertained, but in general most East Indiamen were required to carry 22 Nine Pounders and 4 Four Pounders as a minimum. On 3rd June he came up with Sir Edward Hughes and Sir Edward Vernon with five ships of war and at the same time, *Egmount* left the convoy for Bengal. On 8th June he "read prayers to the people".

The 25th June saw his passage through the Indian Ocean completed when he arrived at Madras. This was followed by calls at Masulipatam (24th July), Culpee (7th August) and Ingeli (23rd December). On 29th December 1777, whilst on passage from Ingeli to Madras he encountered a fierce storm and struck a sand bar. His main and mizzen masts were split and had to be cut away and as there was a danger of foundering, the boats were swung out. Guns were fired and false flares shown, and at dusk the Indiaman *Troughton* arrived to render assistance.

Captain Ogilvie sent forty of his non-essential crew over to *Troughton* 'out of harm's way' leaving just enough on board *Valentine* to man all of the pumps. The following day, a large portion of the *Valentine's* cargo was laboriously loaded into the ship's boats and taken ashore, in order that the ship might be lightened. On 2nd January 1778, *Troughton* sent over 30 sailmakers, carpenters and seamen to help in the rescue. Eventually the ship was got on to an even keel, and jury masts rigged. As many leaks were stopped as could be located and then kedge anchors were laid out to seaward, thus enabling the vessel to be warped off the rocks.

Valentine staggered on to Tranquebar which was reached on 24th February, enabling some elementary repairs to be made. On 22nd March 1778, the ship arrived safely in Bombay where major repairs and refitting could be undertaken as well as unloading cargo and taking on board cargo for England. These actions took until 7th June when *Valentine* departed for Madras.

On 25th July 1778, whilst at Madras, Captain Ogilvie writes: *"was sent for to attend the Select Committee who after swearing me to secrecy, informed me of the company's orders to besiege Pondicherry, that Sir Edward Vernon meant to attack the French Squadron for which the assistance of two Indiamen was requested and that 'Valentine' would be one of them"*

Captain Ogilvie immediately repaired on board *Valentine*, informed his officers and gave orders for the gundeck to be cleared of all cabins.

On 1st August 1778, *Valentine* departed from Madras as part of a naval squadron. The log laconically describes this part of the voyage as being *"on a cruise"*.

On 8th August, the Flagship (Rippon?) signalled for all captains to repair on board for a meeting when it was unanimously agreed to fight the French. When the French were sighted, the Commodore made the signal *"Form into a loose line of battle, 'Seahorse', 'Valentine', 'Rippon', 'Coventry'."*

There appears to have been two French vessels and they fired on *Seahorse* and *Valentine* inflicting such heavy damage that the latter was forced to withdraw in "a shattered condition with the ship ungovernable".

Captain Ogilvie wrote in the log:

"Here, I cannot omit without great injustice to all my officers and men to make particular mention of the gallantry with which they received and

sustained the very fierce fire of these two heavy ships and the manlyness (sic) with which they stood to their quarters and fired their guns."

Ogilvie later records 1 European dead, 12 wounded, with 1 lascar dead and a few wounded. The entire episode spanned 30 hours involving the ship being hit in the hull 28 times by 24 pounders as well as by grapeshot and suffering considerable damage to the rigging.

Valentine returned to Madras on 9th September 1778 for yet more repairs which took until 8th February 1779 before she was fit to sail for St Helena where 15 men landed suffering from scurvy. On 25th June 1779, *Valentine* set out for Britain, in company with *Latham, Mansfield, Lord Holland, Lord North, Rockford, Nothington* and *Grosvenor,* all East India Company ships. Ascension Island was passed on 1st July. On 18th July, the convoy met up with and boarded a Portuguese slaver carrying slaves from the Guinea Coast to the Brazils.

Shannon, on the west coast of Ireland was reached on 2nd September and the convoy spent several months awaiting the arrival of the convoy escort, and then for fair weather. On 8th November, the escort, in the form of *HMS Jupiter, HMS Apollo,* four frigates and two cutters arrived in the River Shannon and on 10th November the escort and convoy set sail. It now consisted of *Eastham, Rochford, Mansfield, Lord North, Lord Holland, Grosvenor, Northington*, two French prizes and four whalers together with the escorts.

11th November saw strong gales and cloudy weather. Captain Ogilvie wrote, *"8am Hove to. Have lost sight of 'Rochford', 'Grosvenor', 'Lord Holland', the Frigates and Whalers plus one of the French prizes."* The following day saw the main topgallant sail split and strong northerly winds. The courses sailed that day were mainly SSE.

On 13th November the winds were still from the north, strong, the sky was still cloudy and the course still SE or SSE.

That is the last entry in the log, for on 16th November 1779, *Valentine* was wrecked on Brecqhou and the entire crew scrambled ashore to be subsequently rescued. Although Guernsey sent over troops to guard the wreck, the ship, which had sunk in relatively shallow water, was plundered by Sarkese and it was rumoured that the Sark ladies were the best dressed in the Channel Islands for years afterwards as a result of the recovery of silks and brocades.

No trace of the manifest of the *Valentine* has been found, but it is believed that she carried saltpetre, dyewood, brocades, china plate, lead ingots, cut and uncut agates amongst her cargo. Two cannon were recovered shortly after the wreck, and in April 1794 Pierre Le Pelley, Seigneur, reported to the Commandant-in-Chief, Guernsey, that amongst his armaments, he had a double fortified six pounder procured from the wreck of *Valentine* which had been proved and found fit for service.

The wreck was re-discovered and dived in 1976 and again in 1982. Fragments of Chinese plateware, dyewood and various domestic items being recovered by a local sub-aqua group. Although some cannons were located, it is not thought that any were salvaged.

It is not unreasonable to wonder how a ship, en route from Shannon on the west coast of Ireland to the Downs, could end up on the island of Brecqhou. This was, unfortunately, an all too common fate for ships entering the English Channel in those days. There was only one lighthouse in the Channel Islands in 1779, that on the Casquets. Vessels entering the Channel would hope to sight the light on the Scillies, or perhaps the Lizard, but were often driven much further southward than they reckoned.

When they saw the loom of the Casquets' light and, mistaking it for a light on the south coast of Cornwall or Devon, they would steer even further south thinking, erroneously, that they were now moving into the middle of the English Channel. The tidal currents on the French side would compound the error and before they knew it they would hit Guernsey, Jersey or the French mainland.

In the case of *Valentine*, being unable to "weather" the Casquets, Captain Ogilvie decided to turn around and run for shelter in the St Peter Port Roads. Falling rapidly toward Sark, the main anchors were let go and some of the masts were cut away. All in vain.

The strong north westerly wind, coupled with the fierce tide, drove the ship onto La Neste and its final resting place. A witness is recorded as saying that the wind was so strong that it was impossible to stand upright on the cliffs of Sark. There was also an unconfirmed report that one of the French prizes which was in the same convoy was also lost in the vicinity.

Sadly, Guernsey does not appear to have placed the artefacts recovered from *Valentine* on public display, and they have variously been reported as being in someone's loft, and in the clubhouse of the sub-aqua group. Technically they must belong to the Crown. Whilst not of great historical importance those artefacts the author has seen would make a very interesting display in any museum.

Fragments of Chinese Porcelain
Courtesy of *Valentine* Exploration Group

CHAPTER SIXTEEN

THE LE PELLEY DYNASTY
1730 - 1852

Dame Susan Le Pelley, who lived in a property known as La Perronnerie decided to remain there but to upgrade the house and grounds to reflect her new status. A pigeon house was built to reiterate her sole right as Seigneur to keep pigeons (Droit de Colombier). In 1731 smallpox struck Sark killing over 30 persons, some 10% of the population. Sadly, Dame Susan died in 1733 and was succeeded by her son Nicholas who died without issue in 1742. As a consequence of there being no male descendant, the Fief passed to Nicholas's brother Daniel who then died in 1752. So far, a not very impressive start for the Le Pelleys!

Fortunately, Daniel had a son, Pierre who, being 18 years of age on accession to the Fief, had his inheritance presided over by his mother as Dame. By all accounts she was a fearsome lady and was responsible for a major ecclesiastical dispute.

In 1754, the Dame appointed a new Minister, the Rev. Pierre Levrier to whom she eventually took a strong dislike. Shades of a later Dame, she tried to dismiss the Minister but he refused to budge. Because Levrier had the support of the congregation, La Dame retaliated by refusing access to the room at Le Manoir where services were held. Her case was that the room was her private chapel with which to do as she wished.

Parents were forced to have their children baptised in private houses or, in an effort to get as close to consecrated premises as possible, outside the door of the Chapel. Marriages had to be solemnised in Guernsey. Eventually, complaints trickled back to the Dean of Guernsey who summoned La Dame to Guernsey to explain herself. She refused on the grounds that she appointed the Minister of Sark and thus she could dismiss him.

During this action, Pierre Le Pelley came of age and was ordered, under dire threat of excommunication, to cause Divine Services to be held. One must feel sorry for young Pierre, faced with a choice between the wrath of his mother on the one hand and the wrath of God on the other. He surrendered to the Greater Force and arranged for a Minister from Guernsey to perform Divine Service. Whilst this was underway, Minister Levrier rushed into church and raised the Clameur de Haro, thus bringing the Service to an unscheduled halt. The matter then moved to the Guernsey Court who found for Levrier but now, with the threat of excommunication removed, Pierre's mother brought pressure to bear on her son who in turn conspired with the Seneschal to make Levrier quit Sark. Eventually a new Minister was appointed of whom Madame Le Pelley approved.

The Le Pelleys chose not to live on Sark during the winter but to spend the season in Guernsey. This was a period when the Channel Islands generally were going through a time of relative prosperity, little of which reached Sark which was constricted by the lack of a decent harbour and the rigid system of land tenure which prevented expansion of house building and thus any growth in the population.

Indeed, as though to rub salt into a wound, inhabitants of the larger islands were in the habit of popping over to Sark for the weekend and the Sarkese felt, justifiably, a bit peeved at being at the disposal of richer excursionists. It seems also that "lager louts" are not a new phenomenon because in the 1770's the Sark authorities were complaining about drunkenness by rowdy visitors.

Pierre Le Pelley died in 1778 to be succeeded by his son, also named Pierre. This was a time for dissatisfaction by the masses. The last vestiges of feudalism were fast slipping out of sight in Europe and the Channel Islands and Sarkese in particular were expressing popular discontent. Not far away, the French Revolution was showing that common men, if they united, could overturn the ruling classes. The primary, almost modest, complaint of the Sarkese was that the Seigneur had the monopoly of milling on Sark; all corn etc. had to be taken out to the Seigneurial Mill or sent to Guernsey.

It could be held that of all of the Seigneurial rights, the right to own a mill made most economic sense. There was probably only enough work to keep one mill in business and to have opened up milling to what would now be termed the "free market" might well have resulted in there being no mills at all.

In 1796, one Tenant decided that he had had enough and built his own mill. The Seigneur ordered him to demolish it; the Tenant refused, with the result that he was ordered to appear before the Seneschal. Because the Seneschal was the nominee of the Seigneur, the Tenant felt, not unreasonably, that his chances of a fair hearing were diminished. The arrest of the Tenant was followed by a trial in the Royal Court of Guernsey where it was decided that it was not unlawful for a person to have a private mill purely for his own use providing he did not attempt to carry out milling operations for third parties. This decision cheered up the Sarkese who promptly celebrated by trying to burn down the Le Pelleys' mill.

Further dissent was caused by the implementation of the Corvée whereby upkeep of the island's primitive roads had, from 1585, fallen on the Tenants who were required to give personal labour. It was proposed that each household along the roads should contribute to the upkeep and this was passed by Chief Pleas in 1803. Regrettably, the Seigneur used his power of veto which, after another excursion to the Royal Court in Guernsey, was upheld. The arrival of the Methodist Church on Sark, coupled with a lessening of the grip of the Anglican Church all helped to engender a feeling of anti-feudalism. Whilst "times they were a'changing" in the outside world, little change occurred on Sark in spite of local fervour and agitation.

In 1820, Pierre Le Pelley died, to be succeeded as Seigneur by his son, yet another Pierre. The new Seigneur seemed to be taking Sark in hand, for the good. A new church started by his father was completed and he masterminded a new school to be built on land that he had donated to the island. It did not last long. A dispute between him, the island and the Royal Court in Guernsey over building a new prison soon stirred up the old antagonisms.

In 1833, a hint of untold riches arrived on Sark via the person of a mining surveyor named John Hunt. Sark's brief flirtation with the industrial age has been described in a separate chapter on the silver mines. In March 1839, Pierre Le Pelley was drowned en route to Guernsey and his brother Ernest became Seigneur. Ernest Le Pelley soon found that he had inherited not a silver mine, but a bottomless pit which swallowed up vast amounts of capital. He borrowed money, he re-financed loans. His brother, by commuting certain seigneurial rentes for capital sums, had greatly reduced the Seigneur's rental income. In 1844, he "bet the farm" by mortgaging the Fief of Sark to one Jean Allaire, a Guernseyman of some financial substance, in the sum of £4,000. This new injection of capital followed the rest of the money into the black hole on Little Sark. He died in 1849, no doubt completely broken by a financial disaster unparalleled in Sark history.

Ernest's son Pierre inherited the bankrupt Fief in 1849 but, being unable to meet the obligations under the mortgage, Dame Marie Allaire, the widowed daughter of Jean Allaire, was compelled to foreclose, forcing the Seigneur to seek Crown permission to sell the Fief. On 4th December, the Fief of Sark was sold to Marie Allaire for £6,000, of which she retained £4,000 for redemption of the mortgage, plus £616 for overdue interest.

Thus the way was paved for the accession of the present dynasty of Seigneurs.

CHAPTER SEVENTEEN

BEHIND EVERY SILVER LINING
THERE IS A CLOUD

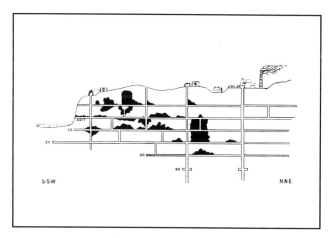

Diagram of the Sark Hope Mine circa 1840

Sark is a geologist's delight. The island, as well as Brecqhou, abounds in many interesting minerals such as syenite, felspar, greenstone, actyonite, asbestos, salt, quartz, serpentine, iron and copper pyrites, hornblende, copper, silver, lead, jasper, agates, plumbago, adamelite, grandiorite, dolerite and mica.

Lead, copper and silver have always attracted attention from miners and there are records of lead having been taken from Sark in the Middle Ages. It was in 1834 that the Industrial Revolution is generally reckoned to have arrived on Sark. A mining surveyor, John Hunt from Chiselborough in Somerset had in 1833 located traces of silver and copper on Little Sark and sought permission from Seigneur Pierre Le Pelley to commence mining. After taking legal advice, the Seigneur gave permission to sink mineshafts on Sark and Brecqhou. Hunt was already looking for copper in Guernsey and was later to move on to Herm. Messrs Johnson & Vivian, in a document entitled, "Report on the Sark Mines (1842)" reported that *at Port es Sais there is a large and promising lode which contains nodules and small strings of iron-pyrites which afford 10 to 15 ounces of silver, per ton"*

Records show that two galleries were opened varying between three to six feet in width. Apart from a passing reference, the extent of this mine seems not to have been mentioned by historians of Sark but the source of this information is impeccable, having been reported to the Royal Cornwall Geological Society in 1871 by the noted mineralogist, W J Henwood.

In order to find the wherewithal to invest in the mines, the Seigneur commuted a number of future seigneurial rentes for capital sums. Miners were brought over from Cornwall and galleries were opened at Le Pot on the eastern side of Sark. Returns from the mine were not up to expectation but in 1836 the centre of attention switched to the western side of Little Sark near Port Gorey.

Thus was born the mine "Sark's Hope" which was on an altogether larger scale than anything seen before or since. An engine house was built, pumps, crushing machines and stamping machines were also brought over from Cornwall. Four shafts were sunk, linking galleries at five levels. Some of the galleries ran out under the sea bed where miners reported hearing overhead, even in fine weather, the dashing of waves and the grinding of pebbles.

The ore was sent by sea to Plymouth, and then up the River Tamar to the Weir Quay Works at Bere Ferrers to be smelted by the

Tamar Smelting Company. This company handled ores from Devon, Wales and even Brittany (the Pont-Pean mine, south of Rennes for example). It is most likely that the ore was sold to the smelting company on the basis of the assay. The assay values varied wildly between 14 ounces of silver per ton of ore to 53 ounces of silver per ton of ore. The price of silver was remarkably stable during the life of the mine, and was generally five shillings a troy ounce. Figures of between 25,000 ounces and 30,000 ounces of recovered silver have been quoted. Pierre Le Pelley was drowned in 1839 and was succeeded by his son Ernest Le Pelley who was faced with mounting problems.

To find the money necessary to fund additional equipment, the new Seigneur mortgaged the entire island of Sark to Jean Allaire of Guernsey. Poor returns from the mine, coupled with the flooding of workings, combined to bring the closure of the mine in 1847.

If it was difficult to get mining equipment to Little Sark, it would have been impossible to get it to Brecqhou. There is what appears to be a disused copper mine on that island dating back to around 1725-1750. Believed to have been worked by some Dutchmen, there are said to be still traces of pit-props and ashes from fires used for cooking.

The mining episode brought employment to some of the Sarkese. Lodgings were required by the Cornish contingent, although quite a few were accommodated in the disused barracks on Little Sark. A modicum of wealth was generated for the average islander as well as the first stirrings of a serious tourist trade.

One cannot help but feel sorry for the Le Pelleys for there was silver on Sark, but in relatively small but concentrated deposits, so arranged by nature, that just as common sense was telling them to shut the mine down, a truly staggering lode would be found. For example, one lode assayed at a remarkable 530 troy ounces of silver to the ton which must have instilled more hope than expectation in the miners.

Ernest Le Pelley died in 1849 and his son Peter Le Pelley found himself unable to meet his obligations under the mortgage and Marie

Allaire called in the loan. She paid the sum of £6,000 for the Fief, from which she retained £4,616 for the debt plus accrued interest and thus acquired the Fief of Sark in 1852.

Two stories have subsequently passed into Sark folk lore.

Firstly, that all of the silver recovered from Sark was lost when the ship carrying it sank off Guernsey. Quite untrue. One of the vessels carrying ore en route for Devon did indeed sink near Guernsey, but this was merely one of many shipments of silver-bearing ore. The amount of silver actually lost would have been minimal and it is possible that the loss fell upon the smelting company which had purchased the ore. Refined silver was never sent from Sark because it never existed there.

Secondly, that tea and coffee services made from Sark silver were displayed in Guernsey to promote the mine. This is highly improbable. The silver once recovered would have belonged to the smelting company. A silver service of some description may well have been displayed in St Peter Port but was probably part of the promoter's armoury of tricks to drum up investors and used time and time again for that purpose. A question-mark hangs over John Hunt as most ventures in which he was involved ended in financial disaster for the proprietors. Some even go so far as to label him a confidence trickster.

Some of the structures of Sark's Hope Mine, mainly a chimney, a ventilation shaft and one corner of the engine house, remain to this day for visitors to gaze at, probably unaware that they are all that remains of the aspirations and hopes of the Le Pelley family.

CHAPTER EIGHTEEN

THE POST OFFICE ON SARK

The Post Office circa 1930

In the eighteenth and nineteenth centuries very few letters were carried to or from Sark and the few that were sent concerned either the Seigneur or the Vicar. It was the practice for local boatmen to transport letters in their fishing baskets and then distribute these at leisure on the beach, unless islanders chose to hunt through the baskets for their mail. Few Sarkese chose to ask for mail, fearing they would have to pay the boatmen.

Seigneur Pierre Le Pelley is known to have considered the idea of a Sark Post Office in 1838. Coincidentally, advertisements were then appearing in Guernsey newspapers indicating the existence of a Receiving House on Sark, with a corresponding one in St Peter Port, whereby letters could be sent to and from on payment of a fee. This would not have been part of the General Post Office, but merely an example of free enterprise which brought the mails from Sark to join up with the universal postal system. Since few Sarkese wrote letters it may be that the "gentry" who could and did write, objected to paying a private individual for a service that might be cheaper if the GPO gained a foothold in Sark.

Events have never moved at a fast pace on the island, and it was in 1857 before the first Post Office appeared on Sark, or to be more accurate, the first Sub-Post Office. This was after a bitterly disputed petition from Chief Pleas to the Postal Authorities. When the subject was first broached at a Chief Pleas meeting it met with universal opposition. Change on Sark was, and indeed still is, viewed with deep suspicion and as a potential breach of the feudal system. The line taken was that if Sark had a Post Office the English Government could and would encroach further upon the rights, customs and privileges of Sark which could result in a complete loss of liberty for the islanders!

After much canvassing and persuasion by Le Pelley, a petition was eventually dispatched to Guernsey. It was said that Le Pelley had a vested interest in having a Post Office on Sark as he spent a lot of the year in Guernsey and wished to communicate freely with his deputy, the Vicar.

On 19th June 1857, Elias Queripel was appointed as Sub-Postmaster at a salary of £3 per year. The first bag of mail left on 21st July 1857. The Office itself was established at La Hèche which already housed a shop run by Mr Queripel. Letters would be posted at this establishment and despite his advanced years, he would walk down to Creux Harbour with the outgoing mail and bring back the incoming mail. There was no door-to-door delivery service so if you were expecting post, you called in on Mr Queripel. This presumably also helped him in his trade of shopkeeper.

It is recorded that in the first six months, nearly 3,300 letters passed through Sark's Post Office. This volume astounded everybody including those Sarkese who had protested vehemently that there was no need for such a revolutionary change to their way of life. The Reverend J L V Cachemaille, that untiring recorder of Sark life, produced a tabulation of the number of postal items which passed in and out of Sark from 21st July 1857 to 31st December 1874.

Instead of being brought to the beach, letters could now be placed in a post box but even this simple task was regarded by the islanders with suspicion. Many were still afraid that the penny stamp would not frank the letter and more payment would be demanded of them if they were seen posting the piece of mail. For months, these persons went at night and by stealth to quickly pop their letters in the box and then run away for fear of being discovered.

In 1859, the sum payable to the Sub-Postmaster was increased from £3 to £11, being the annual stipend of £4, plus £5 for house to house delivery (except to Little Sark) and £2 for conveying bags of mail to and from Creux Harbour.

On 21st January 1868, Elias Guille was appointed Sub-Postmaster and the office relocated to his cottage at New Place. On 6th December 1869, it was reported that the Sark postman had resigned as he would not deliver the mail on Sundays when it was detained by bad weather.

1870 found another change, with Francis Baker taking up office at an establishment in Rue Lucas, close to New Place. In 1890, a new service arrived which must have struck terror into the hearts of the Sarkese. The Sub-office was appointed a Money Order and Savings Bank. To those islanders who viewed the arrival of the post box with suspicion, the thought of handing over hard cash in exchange for an entry in a book must have been the nearest they had got so far to a vision of purgatory!

In 1895, Little Sark had its letters delivered on two days a week, to be later expanded in the summer months. In April 1896, the railway age reached tiny Sark, with its Sub-Post Office being appointed a "Railway Sub-Office". This meant that The London South Western Railway, and later, The Great Western Railway established a "Sark Bag" in their travelling post trains. In 1903, the telegraph reached Sark and a telegraph office opened within the Sub-Post Office from 8.00am to 8.00pm daily and for two hours on a Sunday.

During the summer of 1905, the Post Office in London announced, "Postmasters may arrange for the conduct of a person to an address by an express messenger" and a Mr Henry Turner of Guernsey decided to have himself dispatched to Sark. Having paid 5s.10d. he and a Post Office messenger named William Gurney travelled to the Post Office in Sark. Gurney never left Turner's side throughout the voyage on the *Alert* and on arrival, proceeded to the Sark Sub-Post Office, where the Sub Post-Master signed for Mr Turner. Henry Turner then telegraphed the Postmaster of Guernsey congratulating the way in which Gurney had done his duty and suggested that he was possible promotion material!

This had an amusing sequel in Alderney just before the Occupation, when an Alderney resident unable to get back there from Guernsey as a mere passenger, consigned himself by Royal Mail. Delivery back home was immediate and his wife signed for him at the Alderney Sub-Post Office. The UK Parliament voted in 1952 to terminate this type of service.

In 1910, officials were asked to be more careful with their sorting as letters for SASK (Saskatchewan) were being mistaken for SARK and vice versa.

The first telephones were operated by the army. A public telephone call office was introduced on Sark in 1915 and by 1925, there were two public telephones and eleven private subscribers. In 1920, the postal service was heavily criticised because the steamer to Sark only ran twice a week and only stayed long enough to land and collect mail. On 13th December 1920, letters were delivered at the

Post Office at 12.15pm and recipients only had five minutes if they wished to send an immediate reply. Complaints were made that letters from London to New York only took six days whereas from London to Sark took five days.

In 1925, Mrs H Perrée of New Place wrote to the Postmaster in Guernsey seeking a nine shilling increase in her stipend. She complained that in the winter, mails could be landed at several places depending on the sea state and she had to run halfway around the island to find out where the mails were actually being landed before even contemplating the task of loading and unloading them. This could then involve a climb over rocks or a mile trek up a cliff path. A Post Office Surveyor investigated and confirmed Mrs Perrée's story with the result that she received her money.

The Post Office remained open during the Occupation, although the amount of private mail dropped substantially. Mail boats were extremely irregular and the postmen often sat at the top of Harbour Hill until the Germans told them to go to the quay to collect mail. Post Office stationery ran out, necessitating ad hoc local arrangements. Herm Registration Labels were used, over-written "Sark" and when 1d stamps ran out, 2d stamps were bisected diagonally. Julia Tremayne clearly appreciated the possible philatelic value of this, but failed to secure a specimen for her relatives.

After the Occupation, things very slowly returned to normal. At that time, the Post Box carried the rather enigmatic and possibly unique notice, "Collections, half an hour before delivery commences. One hour before mail steamer sails." On 1st June 1965, Sark had a special rectangular hand-stamp issued to commemorate the Quater-Centenary of the grant of the Charter to Helier de Carteret. From 1st October 1969, the Channel Islands assumed responsibility for their postal affairs and whilst no Sark stamps, as such, were issued, many Guernsey issues have featured an aspect of Sark life.

The absence of Sark stamps is puzzling. There was enough mail originating from Sark to justify indigenous stamps and it would have made the island a lot of money. Indeed, judging by the large numbers of brown envelopes which leave the island presumably in connection with the Sark Lark there was a useful source of revenue waiting to be earned.

The opportunity was missed, or if not missed, then not pressed with sufficient vigour and Sark has had to be satisfied with a percentage of Guernsey's stamp revenue. For an island with no stamps of its own and only one Post Office, the postal history of Sark is a surprisingly full one.

CHAPTER NINETEEN

THE COLLINGS DYNASTY
1852-1927

History may well pinpoint 1852 as the date when everything started to go downhill for Sark. The de Carterets were the colonizers and the Le Pelleys were the consolidators. From thereon, things have become somewhat unravelled.

To put the new dynasty into perspective, it is necessary to go back a few years to consider the Allaire connection. Jean Allaire, according to Dame Sibyl Hathaway in her autobiography, was a privateer who operated out of the island of Jethou (near Herm) which he owned. He was also, she says, of unchristian temper and given to violence and debauchery. In her biography of Dame Sibyl, Barbara Stoney embellishes the story with details of a particularly nasty murder committed at a property known as "The Mount" in Guernsey.

Like everything connected with Sark, questions abound over this man. He died in 1846 aged 83 which makes his birth around 1763. He held the Tenancy of Jethou from 1822 until his death. Although he is reputed to have used Jethou as his headquarters for privateering, the fact is that in 1815 following the Battle of Waterloo, Britain and France were at peace and this was seven years **before** he obtained the Tenancy of Jethou. It is difficult to reconcile the use of Jethou for privateering within this time frame.

In the book, "A People of the Sea", which is a very erudite work edited by A G Jamieson, on the maritime history of the Channel Islands the only mention a Jean (John) Allaire gets is in the table of Guernsey shipowners which shows him to have owned three ships with aggregate tonnage of just under 1,000 tons, The book has three chapters on privateers, one of which lists the names of many captains who successfully took prizes but Jean Allaire's name is not amongst them.

Allaire does not get much of a mention either, in L James Marr's "A History of the Bailiwick of Guernsey". There is in existence a journal of a voyage Allaire made to Buenos Aires around 1803-05 so there is some evidence of his maritime activities. The incident at "The Mount" revolves around an old lady who is said to have pleaded for the life of her son, sentenced to death for sheep stealing and was rewarded for her pains by being thrown down stairs to her death.

Why the old lady should have considered that an allegedly notorious privateer could have helped her over a question of sheep stealing is not known, but assuming Allaire to have been in his late thirties when this incident occurred, it is not likely that a person could commit a murder in Guernsey in or around 1800 and not be brought to account for it.

The conclusion one is forced to accept is that whilst Allaire undoubtedly existed, his personal curriculum vitae has been embellished somewhat by Dame Sibyl to add a little colour to her family's otherwise drab history. Indeed, this is only one of a number of episodes which have been "embroidered" by La Dame.

In 1844 Jean Allaire lent £4,000 to Ernest Le Pelley to enable the latter to further exploit the silver mines on Sark. This raises another question mark, for the Crown was always very keen to know to whom the Fief of Sark was going to be mortgaged and it is hardly likely that the Crown Officers in Guernsey would have recommended that Le Pelley be allowed to borrow money from a notorious privateer knowing, that in the event of default, the same person would have some four hundred persons in his thrall.

Two years later, Allaire was dead. Jean Allaire had two children, a son who committed suicide some three weeks after the death of his father, and a daughter, Marie. Thus, even before the estate had been evaluated the son had died and Marie inherited, amongst other things, the mortgage from Le Pelley.

Marie Allaire-Collings was a widow, having been married to Thomas Guérin Collings who had died in 1832. Marie, at the age of 61 became Dame of Sark in 1852 but sadly, she died in 1853 and the Fief passed to her 25 year-old son, the Reverend William Thomas Collings. The Collings family were from the West Country but had lived in Guernsey since around 1735. The Guernsey branch merited an entry in Burke's Landed Gentry for a short period during the 1860's but the Sark Collings were very much the junior branch of the family. Until obtaining the Fief of Sark by purchase, the Collings had no connections with Sark whatsoever.

There then arises another example of curious acts of "needle work" by Dame Sibyl. In her autobiography, she comments that the Reverend Collings had at one time been Canon of Wells Cathedral, which is quite remarkable progress through the ranks of the clergy for a twenty-five year old! In fact, the "Directory of Clergy" for 1850 does not show him as being in Holy Orders at all in that year. The 1853 edition shows him as being one of two curates at St Cuthbert's Church in Wells. The vicar of St Cuthbert's, the Reverend H W Barnard MA was, however, one of the four canons of Wells Cathedral, so perhaps this is how the myth started.

Be that as it may, William Collings assumed the mantle of Seigneur in April 1853 and the new dynasty had arrived. He remained in the old Le Pelley residence and added a tower from which to look out towards Guernsey. Like the Le Pelleys he crossed to Guernsey to live during the winter months.

He turned his attention to the island's Militia, a military body which has been extensively described in the book, "The Royal Sark Militia" by Bethia J Hurden. It is sufficient here to state that it had vague origins in the original forty Tenants and gradually evolved until in 1744 it numbered some 100 men and took shape as an army unit. The Reverend Collings assumed the rank of Lieutenant-Colonel which may seem rather grand until it is realised that in those days, to qualify as an officer of the militia, property qualifications were more important than military experience. In fact, to become a Lieutenant-Colonel, it was required that the candidate "*should be seized or possessed of an Estate with a yearly value of £600*" which Sark probably yielded.

It is not unknown for reverend gentlemen to dabble in worldly affairs as an adjunct to their vocation. In the twentieth century, steam railways seem to attract clerics in droves and doubtless Collings had an affinity towards military matters and probably enjoyed being the Grand Old Duke of Sark. It would not have done the Sarkese any harm either to have received a spot of military discipline.

From about 1850 onwards the number of tourists increased and the income from this source became a major factor in the Sark budget. The "romantics" such as Swinburne and Victor Hugo visited Sark and having written about the island, others in turn came to see Sark for themselves.

In 1882, the Reverend William Collings died and was succeeded by his son, William Frederick Collings who was a completely different kettle of fish. Probably as a reaction to the influence of his father he rebelled against both Church and the Militia. As regards the former, he had an almost pathological dislike of clergymen and of the latter, he allowed Sark's little army to fade away and die.

William Frederick Collings embarked upon a long crusade and feud with the minister, the Reverend Louis Napoleon Seichan. Nobody knew the real reason for the dispute; some said that the Seigneur objected to the Order of Service in the church. Others say that Seichan was accused of selling the copper stoves from the church for their scrap metal value. In fact, it was probably as a result of the high moral tone Seichan took towards Sark's immoralities.

It did not stop there. Abusive slogans were chalked on rocks around Sark. Collings was in the habit of riding his horse at the Minister, terrorising the Minister's wife to the extent that she was forced to seek refuge in a local hotel and firing his gun on public highways in the presence of the Vicar. Indeed, Court records indicate that he had appeared as a defendant to answer charges of assault, wounding, threats, insults, slander, libel and breaking into a dwelling house. In 1893, he was committed to prison in Guernsey for four weeks. Seichan had been Chaplain to the French penal colony of Devil's Island and he surely must have felt that he had leapt out of the frying pan into the fire when he arrived on Sark.

Collings' violent moods were not restricted to outside the home and Dame Sibyl's autobiography contains accounts of threats and violence meted out to her. Indeed, on one occasion, such was her fear upon being turned out of La Seigneurie in her nightdress, that after taking refuge with a friend, she boarded the steamer to Guernsey and thence travelled to London to get married to her sweetheart.

In 1912, Collings was again in prison, this time for threatening to shoot a reporter. It seems that a Mr Lovibond tried to defend Sibyl's younger sister Doris from violence from a drunken Collings, only to find himself at the business end of the firearm. Both Lovibond and Doris fled to Guernsey, pursued by Collings, whereupon he was arrested. After a trial, he was bound over for twelve months on his own recognizances.

Collings died in 1927 and it is difficult to point to any major advance in Sark which could be attributed to him. Although his stewardship lasted forty-five years it was the effect of outside events and influences which moulded Sark into the island Sibyl Beaumont inherited on 20th June 1927.

CHAPTER TWENTY

CORKS AND PENNY REDS

One of Sark's more notable residents was the artist, William A Toplis. Born in Sheffield in 1857, he came to Sark with his wife in 1883 at the age of 26 for a holiday, and by the time the holiday was over he had decided to stay. Already he had paintings accepted by the Royal Academy and obviously found Sark to his liking both for the clean air, the good light and remarkable scenery.

Perpetually short of money, but with the apparent backing of well-connected people, Toplis was able to live "on tick" until paintings were sold, at which time debts were paid off and a new round of credit started. Like most artists, he was a trifle eccentric and this did not endear him to the Sarkese who regard anyone out of the ordinary with total suspicion. Toplis was also a fully paid-up member of "the awkward squad" and took a delight in rubbing up the wrong way those in authority. Since "authority" was represented by the Seigneur, and since on occasions, the Seigneur was Toplis's landlord, this meant evictions and harassment.

Things became worse when, in 1896, the Reverend Louis Napoleon Seichan was appointed Vicar of Sark. Appalled at the immorality he found on Sark, Seichan immediately began to campaign against extra-marital, pre-marital and under-age sex. This put him into immediate opposition with the majority of Sarkese who undoubtedly felt that such goings-on were part of the "perks" of life on

Sark. Toplis incurred yet more wrath from Seigneur Collings because he befriended Seichan but even more alarming, he made a mortal enemy of one Thomas Godfray, the Seneschal.

If Toplis was a member of the "awkward squad" then Godfray was its divine head. Godfray was in fact the leader of Sark, even though the textbooks indicate that the Seigneur is Lord of the island. Out of the 40 votes available to be cast at meetings of Chief Pleas, it was reckoned that Godfray could call upon 21-23 votes by a complex network of brothers, cousins and close friends, not to mention a bit of gerrymandering. As Godfray was also the Judge and Jury at the Sark Court, Toplis really had shot himself in the foot.

A conspiracy was hatched to drive Toplis from Sark. Eviction notice followed eviction notice. Prospective landlords were warned off from letting property to the artist; most obeyed, but some brave souls created tenancies of varying durations. When summoned to appear in court, proceedings were conducted with a blatant disregard for legal procedure. Toplis invariably lost. Shots were fired into the Toplis home, domestic pets were killed and windows broken without any action being taken by the so-called forces of law and order.

Muriel Toplis, a daughter, was taken to Court for passing along a private road to collect water. She was not allowed to swear the oath, being told by Godfray that the word of a landowner was worth more than one of a mere girl. Godfray kept repeating that it was impudent and impertinent of her to use the path, not as comments used in summing up, but whilst the trial was ongoing which shows that he hardly applied his judicial mind in an impartial manner!

The start of the Great War brought some respite to Toplis from persecution by the Sark authorities although he was now becoming a bit of a hermit and a trifle anti-social, and who could blame him? He took it into his head to collect the corks washed up on the beaches of Sark and by the time the war ended had amassed some fifty three thousand specimens. Why he did this will never be known; what happened to the corks is also a mystery.

Toplis was obsessed by the adjacent island of Brecqhou. He realised that something about it was not quite right, and correctly determined that it was not part of Sark, but that it had been annexed by earlier Seigneurs. He planned secret underground quarters for the island, from which he could mine silver and live in secretive comfort with his family. Efforts to obtain Brecqhou, however, were unsuccessful, it having been let to George Sharp for 50 years from 1911.

Toplis had been a keen stamp collector since the end of the previous century and had decided "plate the Penny Red". This famous English stamp was produced by means of printing from engraved plates. Each plate was numbered and the plate number was incorporated into the margins of the stamp. In addition, the position of each stamp within the confines of the sheet was indicated by the use of two letters in the top left and right-hand corners respectively. Thus stamp AA was the top left-hand stamp of the sheet. Stamp TL was the bottom right-hand stamp of the sheet. Each sheet had 240 stamps and, there being 151 different plates, a total of 36,240 different versions of the same stamp were possible. Each plate was used for very many printings; indeed, they were not replaced until serious wear had occurred.

It was Toplis's ambition to re-create all 151 plates, by collecting one specimen of each of the 36,240 stamps. Given that he was living just about as far away from the mainstream of stamp collecting as it was possible to be, he looked to be on to a loser. Not so. By 1903, Toplis had amassed some thirty-three thousand penny reds and had managed to complete 45 complete plates. (It has to be realised that in trying to track down each one of 36,240 different stamps, Toplis amassed a considerable number of duplicates).

His old enemy Seigneur Collings died in 1927 and was succeeded by Sibyl Beaumont but Toplis soon fell out with her and her new husband, Robert Hathaway. When the Germans took over Sark, he claimed that Dame Sibyl should forfeit the Fief on the grounds that no effort had been made to resist the occupation but in this he was legally incorrect, since the entire Channel Islands were surrendered upon instructions of the UK Government.

The Occupying Powers tended to respect Toplis and never attempted to steal either his pictures or his stamps. That, it seems, was left to others after hostilities ended. Toplis died in 1942 aged 85 and his wife in 1944. After the war, the true value of the stamp collections became apparent and in 1962, they were sold at auction in London. It has been estimated that at 1994 catalogue values, the entire collection would have been worth £3,000,000, no small sum for an eccentric!

In 1969, many pictures were stolen from the studio which was then burnt down killing Maggie Toplis, his fourth child, who was inside. The arsonist/thief, and one would assume also the murderer, is said to be known to the Toplis family. Many of the stolen pictures have subsequently been sold on the open market and some have been returned to Sark.

The island of Sark actually owns three Toplis paintings, two of which are stored in the Candie Museum in St Peter Port. The third is alleged to be hanging in a private residence which, if correct, does seem rather irregular. Ownership of these paintings, which must be worth a considerable sum, is not recorded in the audited accounts of the island of Sark.

OLD SARK DANCE

The Dance of the Hats

Three hats are placed on the floor for
each set of dancers.
The leader of each set circles the end hat
and picks up the other dancers to weave
a figure of eight in and out.
Now the second dancer leads.
The step is a kind of shuffle and stamp
with a very marked rhythm.
It's a very old dance; nobody now
knows what it means!

CHAPTER TWENTY-ONE

RADIO SARK

Sark was intended to be the scene of a very interesting experiment in 1913. Whether it came to pass, or whether the intervention of the Great War put paid to it, is not known. Certainly in that year, active preparations were being made by Post Office engineers to connect Guernsey and Sark by means of the new wireless telegraphy, the invention of the "Italian gentleman, Mr Marconi". Having recently sent a message eight miles across the Bristol Channel using "electrical forces", Signor Marconi was keen to take on a bigger challenge.

The earliest broadcast reference to Sark located so far, is a play transmitted in 1929 by the much lamented classic programme "Children's Hour", from stations 2LO (London) and 5XX (Daventry). Two children, in the best traditions of that programme, thwarted French-inspired plans to capture Sark as a springboard for invading the UK. The sound effects, feet on shingle and waves dashing the rocks, were reported as being "admirably imitated".

In late 1931, one of the sons of La Dame decided he was going to have a wireless broadcasting station constructed on Sark. When complete, it was the intention to place this at the disposal of the British Government, doubtless for a small consideration! He duly wrote to the Postmaster-General announcing his intention and was politely informed that under the Wireless Telegraphy Act of 1904, all concessions for the establishment of wireless stations had been granted to the BBC.

Young Beaumont appeared to think that being a possible Seigneur-elect of Sark he could do exactly as he liked, and he pointed out that the Wireless Telegraphy Act did not apply to Sark. In support of this claim, he stated that none of the inhabitants of Sark who had radios had ever taken out the necessary wireless licences.

It appeared that when the 1904 Act was sent over to Sark for registration it was ignored and never registered at the Greffe Office. By May 1932, the Act had been duly registered and it was reported that the Seigneur and one other person had taken out licences and that a further four offenders were expected to follow suit shortly. Fortunately, Sark was forgiven and has had its fair share of radio coverage since then and nowadays the inhabitants must surely pay their television licences promptly.

In 1937 there was broadcast a 15 minute talk about Sark by Hugh Norman. This seems to have whetted appetites, for in 1938 the BBC in Bristol contemplated something altogether more ambitious. It started with a formal letter from the producer, Francis Dillon, to Dame Sibyl Hathaway seeking permission to make the programme. On 4th April 1938 Sibyl gave her gracious consent in a letter from which the following extract is worth reproducing here:

"It will not be easy to get people to talk, but I think that if you can give me some idea of what you want, I can get some of them together to rehearse the old patois songs to the accompaniment of an accordion. I will give you a short talk on the history of Sark as you suggest, naturally I could not think of any remuneration for myself, I am only suggesting it for the peasants."

This last phrase is a revealing insight into the mind of La Dame. Her letter was a formal response to a formal request from a man she had never met before. It was not a jocular reference to the natives of Sark by one person on friendly terms with the other. It has to be taken at its face value, insulting and derogatory to the people of Sark, her people.

The formalities completed, preparations were soon underway. However, the BBC were quick to find out that going to Sark to record a programme was not quite the same as motoring out to Windsor, for example. The "van" used for recording weighed over seven tons and it was calculated that if it were placed on a Sark boat, it would surely sink it. There seemed to be no alternative but to ship the "peasants" over to Guernsey and do the recordings there. This meant boat fares and hotel accommodation and the projected cost of the venture was now mounting, much to the consternation of the BBC accountant back in Bristol.

Francis Dillon duly arrived on Sark and obtained lodgings at the Galerie Serquiaise which proudly proclaimed that it held "Exhibitions of Fine and Applied Art, was a Café-Dansant and gave Club Privileges for Subscribers." More importantly, from Dillon's viewpoint, there was a telephone, Sark 36.

Dillon's first report back to Bristol was cautious:

"There are certain difficulties with these speakers and singers. There is a mass of songs on the island which the Sarkese claim to be folk songs, but a large number of these are merely 19th century vaudeville recollected in tranquillity. It will take the best part of two days' work to sort them out. Some of the Sarkese speak no English, one of the few remaining silver miners for instance".

Clearly someone was having poor Dillon on! Silver mining operations ceased in 1847, some 91 years prior to this report. Even if a boy went down the mines at the tender age of ten he would have been over 100 years of age in 1938! No further reference to interviewing old miners arose.

Dillon did suggest that the Sarkese used for the singing and the speaking parts should be paid sums ranging from five shillings (25p) to ten shillings and sixpence (52.25p), with the sum of one guinea (£1.05) reserved for unspecified "notabilities".

91

Events were gathering momentum and on 23rd May 1938, recording equipment which was light enough to be loaded on to the Sark boat was located. The question of charging the batteries then presented some difficulties. Dillon explains that if the work were done on Sark, it would be a long job and suggests that the Belgrave Motor Works in St Peter Port should be entrusted with the task.

He then made the plaintive (but unanswered) question, *"If I can speak in a tiny meek voice, may I ask why the bloody things cannot be charged in London?"*

We now see some signs of the eternal struggle between the early "luvvies" and the technicians who actually made things work. Dillon writes:

"There will be accommodation for two ordinary engineers, one super engineer and one of "them" at three different levels of expenses. I will give them a short lecture on the merits and economy of each when they arrive. Then they can pick for themselves. There are too many snags to make hard and fast bookings for this sort of spoilt darling."

Events moved on. By 28th May, Dillon reports back as follows:

"I had of course made a most elaborate recording schedule for the 3rd to 8th June carefully dovetailing in the various Islanders, who for some curious reason, earn their own living by fishing and farming. Often this takes them out to sea or across the Island for hours at a time."

The man from the Beeb obviously was still very much on a learning curve as far as Sark was concerned!

The question of charging the batteries arose again, with the suggestion that it could after all be done on Sark. It would take at least 18 hours and the batteries would need to be dispersed to various charging points around the island. However, as Dillon says, *"18 hours is as nothing in the life of a Sarkese."*

Dillon really had the welfare of his troops at heart for he then issued the following sardonic advice:

"It might be as well to tell the engineers to bring their own hot water bottles and nightie cases. Sark is a bit stark for shops. I had to get my hair cut

by the lighthouse keeper who wrapped me all about in a Trinity House flag. The quickest way to get seasick pills is to write to C. Stonelake, Chemist, Smith Street, Guernsey and enclose 6d per pill, plus twopence for postage. One pill lasts twelve hours but of course only for one person get four!"

At long last all was ready, and listeners to the National Programme in early 1939 would have heard the programme entitled, "Welcome to Sark" open with these words from Dame Sibyl:

"Sark is the last independent feudal state in the world, and as Dame de Serk, I owe homage to the Duke of Normandy, at present his Majesty King George the Sixth, descendant of William the Conqueror. I hold the island under a grant of Queen Elizabeth made in 1570. That grant was made to accord with the ancient Norman Feudal system, and that system is still in force in Sark. We make our own laws and the rights of the Seigneur have never been annulled. My Tenants are fishermen and farmers and you will hear how they live and how they are ruled."

She continued:

"Our patois has never been written down. It is a spoken tongue only, a pure derivative from the old Norman French. When we conquered England in 1066 we took the language there. We brought it here from the parish of St Ouen in Jersey in the year 1565."

When one considers that she was descended from a family who only acquired Sark in 1852 by the foreclosure of a mortgage, that moreover, this family had connections with Guernsey from only 1735 and before that were of West Country origin, one might have been forgiven for thinking from her talk, that she had personally landed at Pevensey at the side of William the Conqueror!

A fact possibly never previously recorded before as far as Sark was concerned was that the incidental music, the "Sark Suite" was especially composed by Arthur Bliss, who in 1950 became Sir Arthur and in 1953, was appointed Master of the Queen's Musick. Historians connected with the work and life of Sir Arthur Bliss have no record of the "Sark Suite" but it is known that Bliss loved Sark and was a regular visitor in the 1950's. In 1965 he composed a special anthem, "O give thanks unto the Lord" for the Quater-centennial celebrations of the 1565 Charter.

There was a sequel to this broadcast. Francis Dillon was alleged to have used part of the Galerie Sercquiaise which was not covered by a letting agreement. The Galerie was run by a partnership consisting of Eric Drake and Vanessa Pennell, a forceful lady by all accounts. Shortly after the broadcast, Pennell commenced actions against the BBC for £20 rent which she alleged could have been earned had the BBC not over-spilled into her property. There followed sheaves of letters, claims, counter-claims and threats of legal action. The commencement of hostilities with Germany did not put off the persistent Vanessa, because the letters continued thick and fast. Eventually, with considerable misgivings the BBC appears to have paid up.

Dillon reported that La Dame viewed Vanessa with considerable disfavour because she never paid any amounts due and was actually considering forbidding her to land on the island. In the event, Hitler intervened and the matter faded into history.

Sarkese heard in the broadcast were La Dame de Serq, William Carre, Seneschal de Serq, Bertie Falle, Fred Baker, Philip Guille, Philippe Hamon, Walter Vibart, Hy Carré, Mai Carré, W le Feuvre, H le Feuvre, John Baker and W H Carré.

Subsequent BBC programmes were:-

1946 - Old Customs of the Island of Sark
1948 - Visit to Sark - Brian Vesey-Fitzgerald
1949 - In Town Tonight - Sibyl Hathaway
1949 - Royal Visit to Sark
1951 - In Town Tonight - Sibyl Hathaway
1956 - A Great Day on Sark - Diana Cartwright
1956 - Island of a Hundred Bays - Leonard Clark
1957 - Origins of the title of Seigneur - Sibyl Hathaway
1958 - Have a Go - Wilfred Pickles
1963 - Sark Remembered - Woman's Hour
1963 - Gardeners' Question Time
1968 - Sark and the visit of Princess Alexandra
1971 - Desert Island Discs - Sibyl Hathaway

Finally, it was recorded that in 1958, the programme "Have a Go" left the Sarkese richer by £14.15s.0d, being the monies handed to the contestants by "Mabel at the Table".

CHAPTER TWENTY-TWO

THE BEAUMONT / HATHAWAY DYNASTY

With the best will in the world, it is impossible to contemplate the reign of Dame Sibyl as being the halcyon days of Sark. Indeed, in examining the events of her "reign" and the various articles and books written about her, it is easy to conclude that she was a thoroughly unpleasant and wicked lady.

To start with it is debatable whether Sibyl Beaumont should have inherited the Fief of Sark in her own right rather than jointly with her sister Doris. It must be remembered that although Sark prides itself on its Norman history, its Charter was a fairly standard English Manorial grant. Very few English Manors gave the eldest daughter preference. The great majority held that if there were no sons, the inheritance was to be shared equally between all of the daughters. Of course, what subsequently happened in such cases was that one of the daughters "bought in" the shares of the other co-heiresses so as to form some coherent estate of property. Dame Sibyl seemed to have relied upon the Laws of Primogeniture.

It could be held however that the Letters Patent of 1611 (which reinforced primogeniture on Sark) applied only to the Tenants of the island. The Seigneur, being a step up the social ladder as it were, followed "knightly custom" in which case the co-heir rule applied. However, when Mrs Sibyl Beaumont became La Dame, she already had her "tanks on the Seigneurie lawn" and took over unopposed.

Thus on 20th June 1927, Mrs Beaumont, a widow with six children became, for better or for worse, the Mistress of Sark. One has to feel certain initial sympathy for her. Her marriage to Dudley Beaumont was clearly a love match and his untimely death from Spanish influenza in 1918 would have been a mortal blow to a less strong woman. The Beaumonts had returned to Sark in 1913 to live at La Valette. Although somewhat reluctant to move to Sark, Dudley Beaumont commenced to put down roots on the island. In March 1913, for example, he applied to the Royal Court of Guernsey for a licence to import bees and in June of the same year his furniture etc. arrived under the direction of Messrs I C Fuzzey of Guernsey. Three lift vans were hauled up Harbour Hill, each requiring seven horses. A commentator of the time remarked on the kindness with which Sark drivers treated their horses and added that it was a pity some Guernseymen could not follow their example. In 1918, just before he left Sark for the last time, he wrote to the Postmaster of Guernsey seeking an additional mail service for the island.

Dudley Beaumont died in 1918, one more victim of Spanish 'flu which swept Europe killing some 21 million, and Sibyl was left alone, aged 34, with five children and a sixth on the way. Her subsequent adventures in Germany have been superbly narrated by Barbara Stoney in her biography of Dame Sibyl and it is not proposed to repeat these here. Thus we return to June 1927 and Sibyl's accession as Dame of Sark.

Dame Sibyl's first act was to address Chief Pleas. Was it a coincidence that she referred to herself as "I am only a woman amongst you" when Queen Elizabeth I at Tilbury addressing her troops used the expression, "I have only the body of a woman etc."? Or was it shrewd stage management?

Her first act was to dismiss Dr Lake-Hope the island's medical officer. A hopeless drunkard who carried a stick to rid Sark of snakes (there were no snakes on Sark so maybe he had a point!), he was a complete disaster. According to William Toplis, he operated on

Seigneur Collings without an anaesthetic, which was the cause of his death. Dame Sibyl makes no mention of this so it may be just island gossip. Toplis suspected that Lake-Hope was not a qualified M D and in this particular he was probably correct.

The Seigneurie was unfit to live in and Dame Sibyl was forced to spend a lot of money modernising the place, which had been untouched for years. Whilst work was in progress, a number of foreign cruises were undertaken and it seems clear that she loved the company of persons who, by the rules of the day, were her social superiors.

It was in 1927 that she met Major Jimmy James but by 1928, she had discovered him to be a bigamist and an embezzler and in due course, he was "sent down" for three years' hard labour. Money was very short and her first ploy was to try and reclaim the vicarage. This is dealt with elsewhere in the book.

She then tried to get permission to sell or mortgage Sark but would not tell the Home Office to whom she was to grant the mortgage, or for how much. This scheme was then converted to one whereby she would mortgage the island to her youngest son. The laws of inheritance on Sark are governed by the Letters Patent of 1611, issued by King James I. These dictate that real property can only devolve to the eldest son. As far as Sark was concerned, the reason for seeking the application of primogeniture to the island, was to keep the forty original Tenements intact. It was felt that to divide a Tenement amongst co-heirs would weaken it economically because there would not be enough productive land to sustain more than forty residential units and the musket and ammunition which each Tenant was bound to keep. In addition to the Letters Patent specifying that the eldest son "gets the farm", it further tells the residents of Sark that they must not sub-divide their land either by sale or by mortgage.

This quaint system still obtains today and indeed, over the years, is believed to have caused considerable problems within families when the head of the household died. For example, if the eldest son was a wastrel he still inherited the Tenement. His brothers, however worthy, were often forced to leave the island and seek a living elsewhere. Oddly enough, the Letters Patent do not specify what happens if there are no sons.

Dame Sibyl had fallen out with her eldest son Francis, the prospective Seigneur. To avoid him inheriting the Fief, she devised a plan whereby she was to mortgage the entire island of Sark to her youngest son Richard, with the intention that upon her death he would claim the Fief of Sark by calling in the loan, rather than it being inherited by the eldest son.

This was a clear ploy to avoid the laws of succession which applied to Sark. The Home Office soon realised that this was basically a family dispute but it was never put to the test. She made it up with Francis and in any event, he was killed during the Second World War, so the matter was resolved by fate.

Actually, the proposed plan was flawed. The eldest son would still have inherited the Fief but with a mortgage attached. Even this mortgage might have been disavowed, since the eldest son is supposed to inherit without any encumbrance on his inheritance.

On 5th November 1929, Dame Sibyl married Robert Woodward Hathaway. He was an American by birth but became a naturalised Englishman on 2nd December 1925. This was a happy circumstance because had Hathaway been American, in those days, a wife took her husband's nationality and Sibyl might have had to forfeit the Fief.

Hathaway was said to have joined the Royal Flying Corps at the outbreak of the First World War but in an extensive effort to find his rank, the author was unable to find any trace that he had ever been in the Royal Flying Corps, certainly not as a commissioned officer. Several Army Lists of the period were consulted (until 1st April 1918, the RFC was part of the Army) as well as the Army lists of Canada since he posed as a Canadian when joining up. It is possible that he did not obtain a commission and if this was the case, then tracking him down is much more difficult.

Legally, Robert Hathaway was Seigneur since he acquired the title by right of his wife. However, Sibyl had no intention of retiring to do the housework and it was very much business as normal. Indeed, Robert Hathaway's name did not seem to figure in reports of official functions on Sark. When the Lieutenant Governor arrived, or a new hotel was opened, or the War Memorial was unveiled, whilst La Dame figured prominently, Mr Hathaway was hardly ever mentioned.

Life continued in the idyllic fashion of the 1930's until with a rude awakening, war was declared in 1939. The Channel Islands could not contemplate that the war would affect them, a view shared in England.

However, as the German Army rapidly sliced through France during the summer of 1940, concern was mounting in the Channel Islands as to what might happen to them. Very many books have been written which deal with the Occupation from almost every conceivable angle and it is not proposed to retrace ground already fully covered elsewhere.

In June 1940 the Guernsey Authorities, understandably, had enough to occupy them without having time to spare to consider Sark. It was thus left to Sark to fend for itself. Dame Sibyl Hathaway went across to Guernsey, partly to see what was what, partly to ensure that her daughter Jehanne's 21st birthday celebrations were not impeded by the war and always the opportunist, to buy up provisions from various evacuated establishments.

Having bade her daughter farewell, she returned to Sark to await developments. A special public meeting was called for 23rd June in the island Hall at which Sibyl made a rousing speech. This seems to have worked because no-one was inclined to be evacuated to England.

Sibyl felt confident that she could get the measure of the Germans for as she wrote in her autobiography, *"Moreover, my name and status were included in the Almanac de Gotha which in those days could be guaranteed to make clear my rights and authority when dealing with upper-class Germans."*

This was a rather odd statement, because in the 1938 edition of the Almanac, Sark is only mentioned as follows:-

"Sark par la représentation du peuple (Chief Pleas) de 54 mbres; le Gouv, héréditaire (Seigneur), le juge (seneschal), les directeurs héréditaires (tenants) des 40 districts, 12 deputés élus directement; en outre 3 mbres n'ayant pas droit de vote."

The name of the Seigneur is not mentioned at all and the reference to Sark is quite low-key and obscure, hardly a card likely to have trumped the Nazi ace!

On 3rd July, two German officers arrived on Sark and because there was no transport, they were left to walk from the harbour to La Seigneurie, a tidy step in summer and in full uniform. The two officers were Dr Maas and Major Lanz and after the formalities were concluded the party enjoyed lunch together and they parted on amicable terms. Major Lanz even suggested that should Sibyl encounter any difficulties she should go direct to the Officer Commanding Guernsey. The following day, 4th July, a German sergeant and ten men commenced the formal occupation of Sark.

Twenty-six days later, Sibyl's new-found contacts paid dividends. From the start of the Occupation, retailers were forbidden to sell spirits etc. to the civilian population at large. Almost no exceptions were made. However, on 30th July 1940 her husband, Bob Hathaway, was granted a permit by Dr Reffler allowing Messrs Mackay & Co. of Guernsey, to supply the Seigneurie with one case of whisky and one case of gin per week! On 27th December 1940, this was renewed but in Sibyl's name. This appears to be an unusually generous concession in wartime and certainly not one enjoyed by many other persons.

German Officers were frequent visitors to La Seigneurie and the visitor book bears mute witness to this. They were entertained and being obviously impressed with their reception, they put the appropriate complimentary comments in the book.

Stories began to circulate on Sark that La Dame was

101

fraternising with the enemy. Whether she was or not, we shall probably never know although the matter is far from clear cut. There is some merit in remaining on good terms with the enemy providing the benefits trickle down to the population in general. Julia Tremayne, in her "war diary", clearly indicates that if there were benefits, they certainly did not reach her household.

Dame Sibyl, in her autobiography, comments that as early as mid-1942 the coffee was a mixture of "barley, dried sugar beet and parsnip ground together" yet in December 1943 she was issuing invitations to German officers to come round for coffee. Perhaps she wished them to take a dose of their own medicine!

This invitation should be contrasted with an entry ten days earlier in Julia Tremayne's diary:

"December 14th 1943. I had to go to the German Commandant for a permit for wood today so as to be sure of a good fire for Christmas. This week, our candle ration is to be reduced to one candle a week. Imagine that!"

Dame Sibyl Hathaway "At Home" with Major Fritz Bandelow

24.12.43.

SEIGNEURIE DE SERK,
VIA GUERNSEY.

Lieber Oberleutnant Herdt
Machen Sie mir das Vergnügen
und kommen Sie mit dem
Doktor Dienstag Abend um
8 Uhr zu Kaffee.
Mit besten Weinachts Grüsse
Sibyl Hathaway
Dame de Serk

TRANSLATION

Dear Lieutenant Herdt,
It would give me great pleasure if you
and the Doctor could join me for Coffee
on Tuesday Evening at 8.0.clock
With best wishes for Christmas
Sibyl Hathaway, Dame de Serk

This particular invitation is somewhat puzzling. The date of the invitation was Christmas Eve. Even the Teutonic mind would not normally expect to discuss business during the Christmas period. Thus there was seemingly no administrative need for Dame Sibyl to issue such an invitation. This is reinforced by the fact that in the previous February, Dame Sibyl's husband Robert had been deported to Schloss Laufen in Bavaria. To lose one's husband in February and in the following December invite representatives of the very people responsible for one's loss, around for Christmas drinks seems most odd. The irony is even greater because even whilst the invitation was being written, British Commandos were preparing to embark for a raid on Sark.

The circumstance of Robert Hathaway's deportation was in itself noteworthy. He was American by birth but he became a naturalised Briton. He was legally Seigneur, for on marriage, Sibyl was supposed to hand over all her duties to her new husband. Of course, she did nothing of the sort, but according to Sark law, he, not she, was Seigneur.

It is somewhat surprising that given the slightly ambiguous wording of the deportation order, plus the fact that Mr Hathaway was Seigneur and taking into account Sibyl's amicable relationship with the Germans, some excuse could not have been concocted to allow him to remain on the island. It has been rumoured that she was glad to see the back of him although having one's husband sent off to a German prison camp does seem a bit drastic!

In 1941, a report in some UK newspapers claimed that La Dame herself had been deported to a German Concentration camp as a reprisal for some unruly behaviour by Sark youths. In May of that year, her daughter, Amice, living in England, wrote to The Times stating that she had heard from La Dame that as at 15th March 1941, she was well and at home on Sark. This letter would have gone via Switzerland by means of the limited postal service run by the International Red Cross.

Another invitation extended by Dame Sibyl to the Germans seems a little odd, to put it mildly. On 10th December 1943, she invited Lieutenant Herdt to attend the prize-giving for her German Language class. Pressure was undoubtedly brought to bear in the islands of Guernsey and Jersey for the German language to be taught in schools. To actually go out of her way to teach the language of the occupiers is bad enough, but to invite a representative of the

Occupying Power to attend a prize-giving ceremony for a class of young impressionable children is highly questionable. School prize-givings are traditionally attended by someone of importance, be it the Headmaster or the local Mayor, but to volunteer the presence of a German officer in that role must have been as unwise as it was unnecessary. After all, by December 1943, the writing was truly on the wall for the Third Reich.

Comparison of Dame Sibyl's account of the Occupation of Sark contrasts strangely with other accounts. For example, in her autobiography, she states that she only left Sark once *"because she was afraid that requisitions would be made if she were not there"*. Julia Tremayne's account is full of unopposed requisitions of her neighbours' properties. Perhaps what Dame Sibyl really meant was, "requisition of her Seigneurie" This would square with the stated reason why she left Sark on that single occasion. The reason given is that two British Officers (both Guernseymen) were hiding in her daughter's house on Guernsey. She states that she took food to them and pointed out to them that it was impossible for Sark to provide a boat to take them back to England. She states that "their families were ignorant of their presence", yet one of the officers stayed with his sister and the other with his mother. These would have been Lieutenants Martell and Mullholland who L James Marr reports in his book, "A History of the Bailiwick of Guernsey" actually travelled to Sark to seek help to get to England but were advised by La Dame to give themselves up.

In her autobiography, Dame Sibyl complains of her boredom of continually having to eat lobster, whereas Julia Tremayne went into a paroxysm of delight when a neighbour from the Dixcart Hotel delivered a pan-ready whiting at a time when Mrs Tremayne had virtually run out of food. Given the state of some of the population of Sark, especially the children, one might have expected La Dame to be continually haranguing the Guernsey authorities for a share of what little they had. As it was, she appears only to have left Sark on the one occasion when her family's property was in danger. As private telephones had been removed around 1941, no pressure could have been exerted on the Guernsey Authorities via that medium so personal contact was essential. There appears to have been none.

Some fifty-plus years afterwards, it is, admittedly, very difficult to form a fair judgement of events, especially when one has never been under the jackboot. We do, however, have the "verdict" of the Military Investigation Branch which looked closely at such matters in August 1945 and they had some fairly harsh comments about the behaviour of Dame Sibyl:

> "*The Dame of Sark, Mrs R.W. Hathaway, has also been guilty of friendly and ingratiating behaviour towards the Germans. Major Albrecht Lanz, the first German Kommandant of Guernsey, in his report on the Channel Islands says that when he landed for the first time on Sark, he was very formally and politely received by the Dame, who explained that a large proportion of the Sark people were descendants of the Vikings who came from the far North. After settling official business, Major Lanz and his staff were invited to a good lunch. The Dame was a particular friend of Dr Maas, Prince von Oettingen and General von Schmetow, who were frequent visitors at weekends. At Easter 1945, Zachau Schneeberger and others were invited to a lobster lunch. The Dame of Sark has preserved her property and privileges intact throughout the occupation: her gardens have not even been modified by wartime agriculture.*
>
> *It is difficult to avoid the conclusion that had Great Britain been defeated, such people as Mrs Hathaway would have qualified for the title of Quisling.*
>
> *There is a large number of intelligent people and people of considerable social and official standing who appear to have been very favourably disposed towards the Germans and to have entertained them on level and friendly terms, for example, the Dame of Sark who has already been mentioned. The loyal Channel Islanders feel very strongly that such people should not continue to hold any official positions, nor should they be received at official functions and it is suggested that steps should be taken to this end.*" (PRO HO45/22399)

Why was Dame Sibyl not prosecuted? The only legislation

under which prosecution could have been instituted was the Treason and Treachery Act and it was felt that the specific offences were not serious enough to warrant that. Defence Regulation "A" - (Acts done with intent to assist the Enemy) - could not be used because at the relevant time, the Defence Regulations were not in force in the Channel Islands, having been revoked by the UK in 1941. That was the view in August 1945.

However, as the revocation of the defence Regulation "A" was for obvious reasons, unknown to the Channel Islanders, it was decided to issue a new Defence Regulation in 1945 which, in effect, revitalised the old regulation. In retrospect, it would appear that a preliminary case against Dame Sibyl could have been made.

The views of the Military Investigation Branch must have been accepted by those in authority. In the introduction to Julia Tremayne's book, the present Seigneur, John Michael Beaumont says of his grandmother, **"Her personality gave her the qualities necessary to lead Sark through the trials of the Occupation with the minimum of hardship, qualities officially recognized by the award from Her Majesty the Queen of the OBE and later the DBE"**.

What he omitted to mention was that the OBE was granted in 1949, by George VI and the DBE in 1965 by Queen Elizabeth II. There was nothing for Dame Sibyl in the Liberation Honours list, although both the Bailiffs of Guernsey and Jersey received instant knighthoods.

The war ended with four German officers and 266 other ranks being taken off the island. By 1946, criticism of Dame Sibyl was on the agenda with a particularly stormy meeting of Chief Pleas in January of that year which culminated with La Dame storming out in anger. The following year she endeavoured to re-introduce tithes of cereals for no other discernible reason than in her view the islanders had become lazy and slack. In the subsequent furore which arose, she again made reference to her position as "Leader of Sark".

In 1950 she was once more under fire and during the election campaign for Deputies of the People in that year, much was said about overturning feudal rule. As usual, it all came to naught. The following year, in response to persistent criticism from one of the Tenants, a Mr Henry Head, she managed to have the Reform (Sark) Law 1951 so worded as to legalise her previous illegality of sitting in Chief Pleas when her husband was the Seigneur and she had no lawful right to attend. Head was joined by a Deputy, Hubert Lanyon, a man with a fine wartime record of active resistance to the occupation. Between them they came up with many reforms, some of which have now been adopted, but could get no support because of a general feeling of apathy and the fear of reprisals.

Dame Sibyl openly said that one of her critics was only a Tenant by right of his wife and the other, a Deputy, would not get re-elected at the next election. Since on Sark, the Douzaine supervise the elections, and she was a member of the Douzaine, one wonders how she knew the likely result of a ballot yet to be held!

Both Head and Lanyon eventually withdrew from the affairs of Sark, the former returning to Guernsey. Much needed to be changed on Sark, as it does to this day, but to simple-minded folk, feudalism is thought to be the mainspring of Sark life and anything which tampers with it may bring the whole edifice down. The ruling clique encourage this view as it suits their book to run their business affairs from a legal black hole.

In 1962, Chief Pleas passed a law permitting Dame Sibyl, (and only her) to have the use of an electrically-driven wheelchair because of her arthritis. On the face of it, a very right and proper amendment to the law which permitted only horse-drawn carriages and tractors to use the roads of Sark. Whilst Chief Pleas were sitting, somebody, thinking ahead somewhat, suggested that the proposed law should be amended to cover any other islanders who might in future find themselves in a similar predicament. This amendment was rejected without any intervention from La Dame whatsoever.

Consequently, in October 1965, Chief Pleas met again to consider the case of John Philippe Carre who had spent two years in hospital recovering from two strokes. Chief Pleas, who three years earlier had fallen over themselves to oblige their Lady, now seemed to feel that they ought not to be asked to decide on a case where only one person was affected. Thus Mr Carré's urgent need was referred to the Traffic Committee who met in 1966.

From there the matter was referred to the Crown Officers in Guernsey. Next stop, the Privy Council no less, who were asked to approve the "Invalid Carriage (Sark) Law" which they duly did in late 1967. Thus La Dame got her wheelchair almost on demand by a "special concession" of Chief Pleas but poor Mr Carré had to wait for two years for the consent of Her Majesty before he could take his electric wheelchair outside his home. Whichever way one looks at this, it really was a very peculiar state of affairs for an island which always tells the media that it looks after its own.

In 1969, La Dame came up against an adversary far cleverer than she. Leonard Matchan, the then owner of Brecqhou, could run rings around Sibyl. Granted, he had his own private agenda to advance, such as having a helicopter flying from Brecqhou and keeping a motor vehicle on that island but he could twist Chief Pleas around his finger with clever and reasoned debate.

In the manner which often characterises ladies who cannot get their own way, she announced to Chief Pleas that she was handing over the administration of Sark to Guernsey. Sark was horrified. However, such was Dame Sibyl's high opinion of herself that it did not occur to anyone that such a step was totally outside her powers. The Home Office soon reminded her that she merely leased the island from the Crown, no more and no less.

In 1974 Dame Sibyl Hathaway DBE passed away after serving as Seigneur for 47 years. One of the hallmarks of Sibyl's period as Dame of Sark was the way she elevated Sark from being merely a feudal backwater where the Landlord-in-Chief was the sort of person who under different circumstances would have been regarded as a drunken loon, to a position of a mini-state with her as the unofficial Queen. Indeed, the German occupiers always referred to her as "Königin". Like her long-serving father, Seigneur Collings, it is difficult to point to any major advance introduced by Dame Sibyl. Such changes as have been wrought on Sark have been brought about by outside sources sometimes in direct opposition to La Dame's wishes.

She appears to have really believed that not only was she an owner of land but she was also the owner of people who lived on that land. In her autobiography, she complains that she was expected to entertain all VIPs who came to the island, for which she received no entertaining allowances as did other Channel Island officials. The fact is she was not an "official" and the only expectation of entertainment came from Sibyl herself as a direct result of her odd perception of her station in life. Even her successor regards himself as a "titular head" responsible to the Crown via the Lieutenant Governor of Guernsey when there is not the slightest shred of evidence to back up this proposition.

CHAPTER TWENTY-THREE

THE MOTHER OF SARK

Her death brought profound grief to Sark and to the very many people who knew her, and who grew to love and admire her. The island of Sark lost a person who cultivated a very true affection for all - one whose aim it was to do all that she could to alleviate distress and to bring comfort and good cheer to her fellow men and women.

Little wonder then that so many turned to her for help when other sources had either failed or did not bring about the desired results and none who called upon her went away empty-handed. She was a woman of great courage and fixed of purpose, as must be borne out by her determination to remain in Sark when that island was passing through difficult years. From this time, she emerged triumphant, yet not defiant and her heart kept free from ill-will yet full of compassion.

Sark would indeed have been a troubled island but for her courage and determination to ensure as little inconvenience as possible was caused to the inhabitants during the Occupation and she used every opportunity to belittle the actions of those who were in supreme authority and control.

On a practical side, her complete knowledge of the German language and the time spent in Germany stood her in good stead. She sewed clothes and made toys for the Sark children, she obtained sugar from sugar beet which she exchanged with the Germans for drugs and medicines for the sick. She arose early in the mornings to take eggs from her hens and when the Germans taxed her on this point, she merely said that cockerels do not lay eggs!

But for her good offices, numerous measures would have been taken which would have brought distress and sorrow to a large number of people and the island would have become a much more ravaged place. She was the means of softening many blows which were delivered and also the means of preventing several people who held high office from being deported. She procured food and clothing from devious sources and diverted these to needy destinations. That so much more is not known of her help and succour is because these acts were done without a fanfare of trumpets, quietly and unassumingly. She received no bouquets, no official thanks, much less any recognition for her endeavours.

Descendants of Dame Sibyl Hathaway may well feel a warm glow when reading this, except for one thing. This eulogy refers to Mrs Annie Rebenstorff and not to La Dame. "Annie Reb" as she was known, was the English-born widow of a German officer. Even today she is described by the few Sarkese still alive who actually knew her as "a wonderful lady" and "a saint". Curiously her exploits have hardly been recorded and it is hoped that this book redresses matters in that direction.

Ironically, it was a German who set the author on the trail of Mrs Rebenstorff. He reported to his masters in Berlin that the people of Sark no longer stood by the Lady of the Manor (La Dame) but by another lady who looked after them better (Mrs Rebenstorff).

Mrs Rebenstorff later moved first to Guernsey and then to Jersey, where she died in 1958. It is believed that her ashes were scattered over Sark.

CHAPTER TWENTY-FOUR

SEIGNEUR JOHN MICHAEL BEAUMONT

John Michael Beaumont succeeded to the Seigneurie in 1974 upon the death of his grandmother, Dame Sibyl Hathaway DBE. Little is known of him except the following:

(1)   He was said to be very impecunious upon arrival on Sark, and as a consequence had to convert the Seigneurie greenhouses to produce tomatoes and to let out certain apartments in the Seigneurie grounds to paying guests.

(2)   By his own admission, he has been unemployed ever since.

(3)   He now appears to be a person of considerable wealth.

(4)   He is occasionally seen on television where he quotes an old Sark saying:

"If you do not like it on Sark, there is always a boat to Guernsey leaving in the morning."

Others clearly know him better, or so they would imagine. In a recent publication " A Portrait of Guernsey" by Dr Richard Axton he is variously described as:

The 23rd Lord of Sark
Incorrect! He is the 22nd Seigneur.

"The hereditary head of the State of Sark"
Incorrect! Sark is not a State, but merely one of several islands in the Bailiwick of Guernsey, which itself is not a State but a Crown Dependency.

"For the security and welfare of Sark, he is responsible directly to the Queen"
Incorrect! He has no responsibilities to Her Majesty other than to ensure that the terms of the Charter of 1565, as variously amended, are adhered to. Nothing in the Charter imposes any duty of security and welfare on the Seigneur.

He is described as the "titular head of Sark"
A totally meaningless phrase!

According to Dr Axton's version of the Letters Patent, the Seigneur *"must care for the safety, tranquillity and weal-public of the State of Sark"*
This is complete and utter nonsense! There is no such thing as "the State of Sark" and very obviously, Dr Axton has misunderstood the Letters Patent of 1565. Before granting a lease to Helier de Carteret, the Crown did consider *"the security and tranquillity of the State"* i.e. Great Britain and the *"Public Weal of the islands"*, i.e. The Channel Islands, but the Charter lays no duties upon de Carteret or his successors in title, other than to pay a capital sum of £50, the annual rent of fifty shillings and to populate Sark with forty persons within certain varying timescales.

Beyond that, the Charter is quite silent. Nothing about defence, nothing about muskets, nothing about a duty of care, nothing about being Head of State, nothing about responsibilities directly to the Crown.

Of course, it is always possible that Dr Axton's book was written without the approval of Mr Beaumont, and does him an injustice, but this is thought unlikely.

CHAPTER TWENTY-FIVE

BUT WHOSE FLAG IS IT ?

The rather attractive flag shown above is variously described as the flag of Sark, or the flag of the Seigneurie of Sark. On balance it seems to belong to the Seigneur but like most things on Sark, all is not what it seems to be.

In 1970 Dame Sibyl Hathaway was in correspondence with Mr W G Crampton of the Flag Institute claiming that the Sark flag was over 200 years old. The Flag Institute thought this very unlikely as Sark had no recorded territorial flag.

In 1991 the present Seigneur in a leaflet entitled "Brief Notes on the Seigneurie" referred to the "ancient flag of the island". He also held that the flag depicted at the beginning of this chapter was his personal standard and should not be confused with the Sark flag which is red with two Normandy Leopards *"passant gardant"* in the centre.

Whether the animals concerned are leopards or lions is a moot point; they tend to look identical anyway to the three lions which were part of the arms of Plantagenet kings and which are now part of the flag of Guernsey.

The story often quoted is that the Dukes of Normandy had two lions/leopards on their flag and added a third when they conquered England in 1066. This is quite false because organised heraldry only dates from between 1150 and 1200 by which time there was no separate Duchy of Normandy.

Certain residents of Sark were not very happy about this situation and felt that the flag now described as the Seigneur's own, was the flag of Sark. Always very aware of the views of his people, Mr Beaumont has now, it seems, decided that the flag illustrated is the Sark flag and he will have a newly-designed flag for his own use. This has yet to be seen at the Seigneurie flagpole.

So the people of Sark can rejoice that the ancient flag, in use since at least 1770 is really theirs - except for one thing; it is not ancient, and it is not over 200 years old, having been designed by a Mr Herbert Pitt of the pre-war Flag Circle in 1938 in response to a specific request from Dame Sibyl Hathaway. This is confirmed by Garter King of Arms at the College of Arms in London who can find no trace of any flag of Sark. Indeed, any such flag would have needed Royal approval.

CHAPTER TWENTY-SIX

IF FEUDALISM IS SO GOOD
WHY CANNOT WE ALL HAVE SOME?

When one considers Channel Islanders in general and Sarkese in particular, it has to be borne in mind that although the islands were nominally possessions of the British Crown, England was a quite remote and largely unknown country, separated by two major barriers.

The first barrier was language. Guernsey and Jersey were French-speaking, Sark had its own peculiar version of French. The clergy were, by and large, graduates of the Huguenot University of Saumur and the legal profession were mainly trained in Caen. Very few persons in Guernsey spoke English, hardly any in Sark.

The second barrier was of course the sea. There was no regular shipping line between the islands and England. If one desired to visit mainland Britain, and frankly very few did, one had to hang around until a trading ship was going in that direction and was willing and able to take passengers. The small number who did brave the perilous journey were generally a few high officials, summoned to London for orders, or a hopeful appellant seeking the King's Justice at the Privy Council. A handful, sons of the élite, went on to Oxford or Cambridge.

Indeed, if the "man on the Guernsey omnibus" likened a visit to England as being on the same basis as going to the moon, then a Sarkese would have considered the same journey as equivalent to going to Mars. The most important persons in the narrow lives of Channel

Islanders were undoubtedly the Seigneurs and the most important political system was feudalism.

Feudalism has been described as a system where "everyone belonged to someone and every someone belonged to the King". It had its roots in Roman times where the head man was called "the senior", (the old one). When the Roman empire came to an end around the year 475 AD small barbarian kingdoms arose out of the ruins. The great engineering works left behind by Rome fell into decay, money almost disappeared, there was no strong central government and it was every man for himself. As money was scarce, protection was bought with land and soon nobles found that they had acquired more land than they could manage.

This surplus land was granted to Tenants in return for a promise of service in war by fighting for the Lord and in peacetime by rendering agricultural and other services. The Tenants in turn sub-leased part of their Tenancies. Life centred around the Manor wherein lived the Lord or Seigneur. His aim in life was to extract as much from his Tenants, serfs and vassals as he could, indeed until the "pips squeaked".

To this end, he acquired a large number of "rights", such as the right to own the Manorial Mill to whom all Tenants must come to get their corn ground to flour. He had the sole right to keep pigeons and doves, ostensibly to prevent the Tenants' crops from being eaten, but in practice a surefire method of ensuring that his pigeons were nice and plump when brought to the table! Not all Seigneurs were equal, there was a defined "ranking" system. One of the visible signs of rank was the Colombelle, or dovecote. A top-ranking Seigneur had a full tower, the next down had a "Tourelle" or half round attachment to the house, and at the bottom end a lower-rated Seigneur merely had a few pigeon holes let into the roof.

He had the right of "tithe" or "dime" wherein one tenth of certain crops were given freely to the Lord by the Tenants. Tenants had to provide free labour to cultivate the Lord's own lands, the demesne land. A live chicken for every chimney was often required to be brought to the Seigneur; this right was known as poulage. The right to tax bread and wine was often practised and some Seigneurs even had the right to their own gallows.

The Seigneur often had to give his permission before his Tenants could marry and this led to the fable of the "Droit de Seigneur" whereby he "sampled" the intended bride. As far as can be ascertained, this was not a formal right, but who can say what some less morally-minded Seigneur might have demanded in exchange for giving the happy couple his blessing?

Seigneurs had absolute power, and as is well known, absolute power corrupts absolutely. Actually on Sark, the intending parties to the marriage had to pay the Seigneur five sous tournois for permission, without which the minister could not conduct the service. This was abolished by Pierre Le Pelley.

The Le Pelleys seemed to have had their hearts in the right place for Peter Le Pelley admitted to a writer that in his opinion, "The Lord of the Manor has no right to prevent any inhabitant from building on his Tenement or those possessing houses, from adding to those houses." This was in direct contradiction to the widely-held view that not even a house can be built without the consent and approbation of the Lord and so was a pretty radical statement at the time.

In the remainder of Western Europe, Seigneurialism was in sharp retreat at the time of the Black Death, which so decimated the population that those who survived found that their labouring skills were in such demand as to enable them to obtained far better terms of employment.

Feudalism still exists on Sark for one reason only and that is because it suits an influential minority of the inhabitants to use it as a cover for other more modern activities. To start with, there is a mistaken belief that all that Sark is today can be laid at the door of the 1565 Charter. When one separates the rights attaching to the 1565 Charter, with some of the practices in Sark today, a quite surprising picture emerges.

As a contractual document, no-one can deny the Seigneur's right to occupy the island of Sark as a piece of real estate although it could be argued that the terms of the Charter have been breached in at least one particular in that the annual "rente" is fifty shillings, (or £2.50) whereas for possibly 150 years, only £1.79 appears to have been paid.

The Charter gave Helier de Carteret possession of the island together with all its rights, members, liberties and appurtenances. These four items in practice were valueless when it is realised that Sark was uninhabited prior to 1563 for a period long enough to have had no rights, members, liberties or appurtenances. De Carteret then gained access to all castles, forts, edifices and buildings. Again, a hollow asset, since there were no structures standing on Sark. Ruin material and fragments of edifices were his so he did at least have a supply of old stones. He was a little luckier when it came to the lands, meadows, feeding, pastures, commons, wastes, void ground, waters, watercourses and ponds. He was a trifle unfortunate as regards woods, underwoods, coppices and fishponds for Sark was very short on standing timber. His fortunes revived a little with his right to rents, reversions and services but became a veritable "no-no" when it came to rights of advowson, presentment, disposition and patronage of the non-existent rectories, vicarages and chapels.

Matters looked up again with his rights to tithes, oblations (gifts for pious purposes) fruits and oblentions although mines, quarries, ports, shores and rocks were a bit of a mixed blessing (as the Le Pelleys were to find out in a later century). The right of shipwreck might well have brought in the odd livre or two. Income from fee farms, knights' fees, wards' marriages, escheats and returned heriot (war) goods together with chattels of felons, fugitives and pirates would hardly have warranted a separate column in the Seigneurial cash-book.

The right of permitting his pigs to graze (pannage), collecting tolls from roads and markets would be virtually non-existent and one might count the number of Ale Fairs held on Sark (to which he had the right of assay) on the fingers of one hand.

The point is that few of the rights which are perceived to belong to the modern-day Seigneur spring from the Charter of 1565. They were tacked on, mainly, in 1583. They could just as easily be "untacked". The insistence that forty Sark Tenants automatically obtain seats in Chief Pleas without any popular mandate is anachronistic. Secondly, the collection by the Seigneur of the "Treizième", for his own personal use, not only has an inflationary effect on land prices but has no impact for good on the island at large. This right was introduced by the Order in Council of 1583 and really is long overdue for repeal. It was not unreasonable to attach to the de Carteret line those rights and customs which that family had long enjoyed in Jersey but to extend this to the Le Pelleys and then to the Collings/Hathaway/Beaumont dynasty is an offence against equity.

To digress slightly, the Treizième is described in most published books about Sark as being one thirteenth of the purchase price, payable to the Seigneur for grant of congé (permission to buy and sell a property). What is peculiar is that one might assume that if the Seigneur got one thirteenth of the purchase price, the seller would get the other twelve-thirteenths. Not so. It appears that on Sark the Treizième means that the buyer pays the vendor the purchase price in full **plus** a further one thirteenth to the Seigneur. A large Tenement recently placed on the market at £1.5m will, assuming it sells at the asking price, increase the personal wealth of the Seigneur by £115,000. It is believed, but not known for certain, that Brecqhou netted the Seigneur something approaching £180,000. The sad fact is that none of this goes into the island's coffers.

Sarkese chant, almost like a mantra, *"Tenements are indivisible"* which is a reference back to the Charter of 1565 which forbade splitting up the Tenements to avoid uneconomic units of land. If the spirit of the 1565 Charter was truly maintained, there would still be a mere 40 houses on Sark even today. However, there are now some three hundred and seventy dwellings, plus hotels and shops on Sark. Thus, in practice, the Tenements are very much divided. However, it suits the Seigneur to maintain that the indivisibility of Tenements is the bedrock on which Sark is founded and if this is abolished, the sky will fall in. The logic is that as he gets a Treizième each time a Tenement changes hands, it is in his interest to keep the value as high as possible. A Tenement where most of the land and the houses were let out on 99-year leases would have little value and thus attract a minimal Treizième. To avoid this, "an old custom" where a lease may not exceed the expected life of the lessor was introduced by Dame Sibyl Beaumont to protect her receipts from devaluation by allowing long leases. There is only one beneficiary from indivisibility and that is the Seigneur. Rather cleverly, he seems to have persuaded his acolytes that it is in their interests also.

The happy absence of motor-cars, aircraft, theme parks, night clubs, gambling casinos and urban blight has nothing to do with feudalism but more to do with isolationism. The same result could be achieved much more simply and certainly more democratically, by a fully-elected island Council. Sark could never be developed to the scale of Guernsey or even Alderney because the limiting factor on any small island is the amount of water available in the aquifers.

On Sark, conservation of drinking water seems to be the last thing on the minds of the inhabitants, because plans are afoot to build a nine-hole golf course on the western side of the island. The water consumption of such a course would be substantial, enough to either seriously deplete the entire water table or pollute it with fertilisers and nutrients.

If such a Council decided to retain the Treizième, perhaps as a kind of stamp duty at 1% or 2%, this would provide funds to ensure that the existing infrastructure remained intact. For example, as far as can be ascertained, the sewage of Sark eventually finds its way, after treatment to only fairly basic standards, into the sea. This is now considered to be a great sin, and one day someone will compel Sark to follow best contemporary practice. Where would the money come from then? Would the Seigneur perhaps hand over some of his past Treizièmes? Let us hope so.

Why then does Sark cling to feudalism? The reason is quite simple - because in doing so, a small minority of Sarkese are enabled to do almost anything they like. The Sark Lark would never be tolerated in a properly regulated jurisdiction. There would be a compulsory safety-net for the unfortunates. There would be an elected Council. There would be medical treatment for all classes of persons. There would be pensions and employment rights. Laws would be certain and not subject to haphazard interpretation by totally unqualified persons. Health and Safety legislation would be enforced. Sarkese would have consumer rights, especially with regard to the building trade.

The thirty or so persons who actually run and control Sark have very cleverly put the myth about that in some way, the nice things about the island - the scenery, the fresh air, the peace and the solitude all stem from Helier de Carteret in 1565 and if feudalism was abolished, all this would vanish. The sad thing is that the other 500 or so residents have swallowed this, hook, line and sinker. To quote a Sark resident of some standing: *"they all believe on Sark that they can do what they like, when they like and no-one can touch them; they are, I'm afraid, a large community of insular people."*

Remembering and defending history is to be commended but there is a limit to how much one can try and ignore the rest of the world. Another part of this book has touched upon the possibility of a Seigneur, present or future, being offered a price for the Fief of Sark which he just could not refuse. Overnight, Sarkese might find themselves with a Seigneur of a thoroughly modern disposition who might regard Sark not as an historical gem, but as a financial or lifestyle opportunity.

In an age when wealth and breeding do not go hand in hand and the term "Noblesse oblige" might well be mistaken for the name of a horse running in the three-thirty at Sandown, Sark may well find itself at the pointed end of the stick. This view may be over-pessimistic, but it does no harm from time to time, to take a long hard look at long-established institutions.

Each Seigneurial dynasty so far has ended with a financial crisis. When the cost of the Brecqhou dispute reported recently in the press to have reached some £1,750,000, comes home to roost, who is to say that it might not be third time unlucky?

CHAPTER TWENTY-SEVEN

THE CHURCH SPIRITUAL

St Peter's Church Sark circa 1925

Without doubt Sark, being relatively isolated and mysterious, would have had its attractions for early holy men and others, seeking a life of quiet contemplation. The first recorded arrival of the Church was in 568 AD when St Magloire arrived with sixty monks. He was a Welshman escaping persecution by the Anglo-Saxons by fleeing to Brittany, then called Armorica, with his colleagues St Tugual and St Sampson.

These three names crop up all over the Channel Islands and in

Brittany St Tugual is believed to have founded a religious settlement on Herm before becoming Bishop of Tréguier in Brittany. St Sampson landed on the eastern side of Guernsey and gave his name to a parish on the island. St Magloire himself became Bishop of Dol.

Legend has it that St Magloire, whilst on a missionary trip to Sark, cured a local Chieftain, (known variously as the Count of Lofesco or Badwall, Regulus of Sark) of some grievous ailment. The prescription was three days of fasting for the chief's family and a bath for the chief himself! It seemed to have worked because St Magloire was given a large part of Sark on which to build a religious centre. Certainly a monastery of sorts was established, for the name is perpetuated today in Sark with the Tenement of La Moinerie. It has been said that St Magloire ran an early boarding school for the sons of well-to-do French nobles, but this is not proved. Sadly, the settlement was wiped out some 200 years later by Norsemen - an event described by a mediaeval scribe as, *"Sark was overrun by heathens who caused much woe and devastation"*.

Around 950 AD, the religious affairs of Sark, along with those of the other islands were handed over by Norman dukes to various monasteries in Coutances, Cherbourg and Mont St Michel. As the fortunes of the warlords and princes ebbed and flowed, so the ecclesiastical title to Sark moved between competing bishops. Mont St Michel one year, Avranches the following year, Coutances another year - all very confusing to the man in the pew! Eventually, some form of stability returned with Sark passing to the Abbey of Montebourg.

In the 10th century times became a little better. The Channel Islands were ceded to Rollo, together with Normandy. Around 1041, William the Conqueror gave Sark and Alderney to one Ranulf in compensation for the loss of half of Guernsey and a little later, both islands were mortgaged to the Bishop of Coutances as security for a loan raised for the invasion of England. By 1000 AD Sark, with a population of over 400 formed, with the parishes of Guernsey and Herm, one of the seven deaneries of the Archdeaconry of Beauptois which itself was one of the four sub-divisions of Coutances.

The "Liber Niger" of Coutances, compiled between 1251 AD and 1279 AD, records shows the parish and benefice as follows:

"Deanery of the islands of Guernsey. The Church of Sark. The Patron is the Bishop of Coutances. The Bishop of Avranches has about two parts of the tithes which are worth about 14 livres tournois and the Rector has the third part and altar fees. Ordinary yearly value 40 livres tournois".

(The Liber Niger, or black book was merely a reference book used to record facts about a diocese for the purpose of administration.)

In 1499 it was decreed that the Channel Islands should be parted from the Diocese of Coutances and enfolded for ever into the See of Winchester.

Sark was extremely fortunate in obtaining the services of Cosmo Brévint as its first pastor. Brévint, a Huguenot exile of no mean ability, made Sark into a veritable model of a Calvinistic community, so much so that the fifth Synod of that Church was held on the island in1570. Cosmo Brévint died in 1605 and an Italian priest David Bandinel was then appointed, who eventually went on to become Dean of Jersey.

Cosmo Brévint was still missed and a rather far-sighted solution was found by the Seigneur paying for the religious education of Cosmo's son Elie on condition that after his training was completed he should reside in Sark and become its minister. In 1612 this happened and until 1674 Elie was responsible for the spiritual affairs of Sark. He was an enthusiastic diarist and in1860 his book of jottings and observations was found in the loft of Le Manoir. This find encouraged a later minister to become a historian of Sark.

It was probably just as well that Elie Brévint kept a close eye upon Sark matters because the Seigneur, now Philippe de Carteret, was busy trying to re-establish the important position held by his family in Jersey. This left little time to attend to the administration of Sark. Philippe was appointed Bailiff of Jersey in 1627 and the following year he had the misfortune to be captured by Spanish privateers operating out of Dunkirk. He was able to purchase his freedom in the sum of £100, plus £17 "expenses".

One area where the Calvinist Church was pre-eminent was the importance it placed on education. A religion which placed so much emphasis on the written word of Holy Scripture would not make much headway if its adherents could not read! Nowhere, in the Europe of the 1600's with the possible exception of Presbyterian Scotland, was the general level of education as high as in the Channel Islands. What was even more important was that schoolmasters were encouraged, indeed ordered, to take particular note of any children who showed promise and to convince their relatives to support and encourage them. Occasionally, the State could be prevailed upon for grants for the very brightest scholar to continue education at an English or French university.

After the death of Elie Brévint, there were a further thirteen Ministers before the next noteworthy incumbent arrived, one J L V Cachemaille who gained the living in 1835. He also acted as Deputy Seigneur when the Le Pelleys wintered on Guernsey, as was their custom. Cachemaille was so fearful of the sea that it is believed that he never left Sark during the forty-five years of his incumbency. It was whilst he lived at Le Manoir that the scrapbook of Elie Brévint was found and this became an inspiration to Cachemaille to research into old Sark records in order to publish the first recorded history of Sark.

In July 1787, the Methodist missionary in Alderney when asked by John Wesley, *"Does anyone in Sark speak English?"* was told, *"Not a single family; had they done so, I would have been over to the island myself"*.

Not withstanding the language problem, Methodism reached Sark and in 1796 a small chapel was constructed at a cost of £300. At this time, Methodism was seen to be subversive if not downright revolutionary, and in 1817 the British Government made £1,000,000 available for the construction of Anglican Churches. This was a very considerable sum of money in those days and is clear evidence of the alarm felt in the ruling circles about the danger, real or imaginary, which the Methodist Church posed. Seigneur Le Pelley obtained a grant of £400 from this fund and used it towards building a new church. The church was consecrated in 1820 and licensed for Divine Service in the following year. The first bishop to visit Sark since the Reformation was Dr Fisher, Bishop of Salisbury who took confirmation services.

The well-known Anglican rebel, Dr Pusey visited Sark when he was suspended from his duties at Oxford and was the first cleric to conduct services in English. He was also the first to wear a surplice, Sark ministers preferring at that time the more austere French garb, and he left this to St Peter's when he returned to England.

Over the centuries, some interesting silver has been gifted to the Church. In 1732, Dame Suzanne le Gros presented or possibly had presented on her death, a silver chalice and paten inscribed, *"A dame Suzanne Le Gros, Dame de 'Ile de Serk et Dependancies, Anno Domini 1732"* (The chalice appears to have vanished). Another item is a silver gilt chalice inscribed, *"Don de Anne Dumaraesq. Dame de St Ouen à Eglise de Serk 1675 August 26"* and a third is a plain hallmarked silver chalice inscribed, *"Don de Mr Robert Selowley à Eglise de Serk 1765"* (This latter item seems to have vanished also). Possibly the missing silver pieces are those in the Seigneurie referred to by the Reverend Bestic in the next chapter.

A further gift, this time of communion plate for use with sick persons, was given by Mrs Louise E Collings, Dame du Seigneur de Serk in 1863 to commemorate three hundred years of settlement on Sark. In 1965, to celebrate four hundred years of the colonisation of Sark, the Parish Church of St Ouen in Jersey presented an inscribed silver chalice and paten.

There are several more recent presentations, generally to express thanks for a life on the island of Sark.

CHAPTER TWENTY-EIGHT

CLERICS IN TROUBLE!

The minister is nominated by the Seigneur. In Presbyterian times, the elders and congregation had a voice in the election, but when Anglicanism was established the Seigneur regained his liberty of choice. He presents his candidate to the Bishop of Winchester, but once inducted, the minister cannot be deprived of his living by his patron. The expense of the services fall on the Seigneur, and during Seigneur William Frederick Collings's reign, instances are found of him trying to divest himself of this cost. For example, in 1886, he "persuades" Chief Pleas to pay £7.10.8d for the cost of bread and wine for Holy Communion. However, the Le Pelleys were also far from innocent in this particular for in 1816 a charge of 3s.6d per year was imposed upon the Tenants for the provision of a lay reader.

Vicars of Sark had a penchant for getting themselves into hot water. In December 1752, Daniel Le Pelley, Seigneur of Sark names and appoints Jacques Levrier, a Protestant refugee from Poiton as his chaplain on Sark and begs the Bishop of Winchester (Bishop Hoadly) to give him Holy Orders and a licence to preach on the island. A couple of years later, Jacques dies and his brother Pierre is appointed by Elizabeth Le Pelley to take his place. By 1754, Madame Le Pelley is disenchanted with brother Pierre and gives him notice that he must leave the curé that Christmas.

Levrier writes to Bishop Hoadly complaining about this and

encloses a letter for a Mr Serrees, the King's chaplain. On 1st January La Dame ceases to pay the vicar's stipend and twelve days later shuts the church. Apart from one service, it remains closed until 1756.

In 1755, La Dame sends officers to evict Levrier who is adamant that he will not leave the manse. Upon his refusal he is summoned before the Sark Court. Meanwhile, the inhabitants of Sark complain to the Dean of Guernsey that although they pay tithes to La Dame, they have no minister and propose to take her to the Ecclesiastical Court of Guernsey. The case was designated, "Michel Simon, Vingtenier, and the inhabitants of Sark v Elizabeth Etienne le Pelley, widow of Daniel le Pelley, and guardian of Pierre le Pelley, Seigneur in his minority".

There then followed tortuous argument involving the Dean of Guernsey, The Bailiff of Guernsey, the King's Advocate and the Bishop of Winchester to try to decide which court had jurisdiction over Sark. It was eventually decided that whilst the Guernsey Court was not the court of first instance for Sark, the Ecclesiastical Court did have jurisdiction over Sark. In the meantime, Pierre le Pelley comes of age and agrees that Guernsey may send over a minister, one Mr Fevot, the minister of Vale to take Divine Service. Pierre Levrier rushes into the church and stops the service by declaring "Clameur de Haro".

On 6th February 1756, a general fast was ordered by the King, and the Ecclesiastical Court instructed the Seigneur upon pain of excommunication to allow a Service to be held in Sark, whereupon Pierre Levrier was allowed to conduct the Service and thereafter to minister unto the Church on Sark. Later the Guernsey Court fined Levrier 18s.0d for his Clameur. By December 1756 Levrier had been absent from Sark for three months having obtained leave merely to go and get judgement about his arrears of stipend. He remained in London on the advice of Lord Granville and Lord de la Warr and other arrangements were made for a minister.

In 1896, another notable cleric arrived, Louis Napoleon Seichen who, as his name indicates, hailed from Corsica. William Frederick

Collings appeared to have a pathological dislike of men of the cloth. For years, Seigneur Collings harassed Seichen by riding at him with his horse, discharging a shotgun near him, assaulting him with a stick, breaking windows in his home, daubing anti-clerical slogans on rocks and walls and terrorising Mrs Seichen. Several times, the Seneschal was able to demonstrate his impartiality by bringing Collings to Court.

Seichan could give as good as he got however. He successfully prosecuted Collings for unauthorised expenditure of the funds of the girls' school, for giving orders to the mistresses and giving the pupils ad hoc holidays.

In 1926, yet another minister, the Reverend Edmonson Nelson Greenhow was appointed. Whereas Seichan had determination and grit to resist the Seigneur's onslaughts, Greenhow had Admiral Nelson's desire to "do his duty". The call came rather sooner than he might have liked. In 1927, Collings died, and having no son his eldest daughter Sibyl Beaumont succeeded him. She was a widow but intended to marry a Major Jimmy James.

When presented to the minister for what was expected to be a mere formality, the Reverend Greenhow had an uneasy feeling that he had met the prospective bridegroom somewhere before. In due course, the penny dropped and he realised that he had not only seen Major James before, but he had actually conducted a marriage service with the Major in the role of bridegroom. This was when Greenhow was in the Far East where he served as a missionary.

It has to be said that the odds against this happening are astronomical and the disbelieving Dame was understandably annoyed when Greenhow broached the subject. However, other happenings were now making her suspicious and it turned out that Major James was indeed a consummate bigamist and was eventually "sent down" at Exeter Assizes.

Always quick to return a favour, La Dame in 1928 served "Notice to Quit" on the Reverend Greenhow, his wife and five children. She claimed not to have any ill-will towards her minister but islanders thought differently. Fortunately, Greenhow had a letter from the late Seigneur Collings dated September 1926, which contained the following clause:-

"And I also promise to pay the said Edmonson Nelson Greenhow the yearly stipend of one hundred pounds sterling for serving the said Curé, to be paid quarterly and to be issuing out of the said seigneurie or lordship of the said island of Sark and also to provide a house and garden which have been usually occupied by the incumbent of the said island."

(Additionally, the Ecclesiastical Commissioners contributed £240 per year.)

Even the Sark Court was compelled to see the injustice which La Dame was trying to inflict on the Reverend Greenhow and he was allowed to both remain at Le Manoir and to officiate as Minister of Sark. Indeed, it was also held that whilst the patronage was in the gift of the Seigneur and had been since 1565, he or she had no power to remove the Living from the incumbent.

The stage was now set for a long-running dispute between La Dame and the Bishop of Winchester, out of all proportion to what was at stake. This is the subject of the next chapter.

CHAPTER TWENTY-NINE

SARK IS A NUISANCE!

So wrote the Bishop of Winchester in 1936 to his legal advisers in London and well he might, for his file on the island of Sark approached 12 inches in thickness.

It started in February 1928, when La Dame wrote to the Bishop stating that *"I am compelled to use Le Manoir, (now temporarily granted to the island Chaplain) as an asset to assist me to support the many public calls of the island for roads, repairs and upkeep."* Her definition of the word "temporarily" is certainly strange, for Le Manoir had been in use as a vicarage for at least 200 years. What was also poetic licence was the inference that the Seigneur was responsible for footing the cost of Public Works on Sark.

Thus not only did she propose to evict the Reverend Greenhow but in future not to provide any subsequent vicar with living accommodation. Furthermore, she proposed to restrict her contribution to the vicar's stipend to £25 per year instead of the £100 previously paid. Her argument was that the tithes only brought in some £110 per year which made the payment of £100 to Greenhow quite a burden.

Because the Sark Court had already held that the existing incumbent, the Reverend Greenhow, had a written agreement from Dame Sibyl's father, both as to the quantum of stipend and the provision of living accommodation, La Dame tried to have Greenhow "promoted" to another living so that the contractual tie would be broken. This ploy failed. Indeed, she accused the Bishop of Winchester of going back on his word on this subject.

Her next move was to insist that the Ecclesiastical Commissioners take over the Sark Church entirely, so that no liability would fall upon her. The core of her final demands was as follows:

(1) No contribution be required of her towards the stipend of the vicar.

(2) She be relieved of any responsibility for non-collected pew rents since 1823.

(3) She be relieved of any responsibility towards the upkeep of the chancel and church repairs.

(4) She be under no obligation to provide a house or vicarage.

Her rationale was that the vicar was in fact merely a private chaplain to the Seigneur and any payment arrangements between them were purely relating to the term of office of a specific vicar. She claimed that she was forbidden under the Charter of 1565 from creating any long-lasting financial liability on the Fief and thus there was no duty on her to pay stipends or provide housing other than at her discretion.

One of the Bishop's legal advisers wryly commented that it seemed rather inconsistent of Mrs Beaumont to ask to be relieved of responsibilities which she submitted did not exist and which in her view had been voluntary contributions from all Seigneurs since 1565. However, being ecclesiastical gentlemen, they all tried to treat La Dame as an honourable woman. They were very reluctant to agree to take on the liabilities of the Sark church until, at the very least, she had accounted for the monies from the sale of pews by her predecessors in title, reckoned to be about £300, as well as all the pew rents (of which more, anon) which she and other Seigneurs had neglected to collect since 1823. Furthermore, they calculated that the removal of these liabilities from the Seigneur would increase the value of the Fief in the event of a sale, and thus La Dame should make a capital payment to the

Church in respect of these relieved liabilities.

These events were duly reported to the Home Office, together with the quite odd intelligence that the Church appeared to be divided into three parts, each owned by a different individual. This latter item of news was received with incredulity in London. When they were eventually forced to accept that the Living in Sark was in the gift of the Seigneur and not with the Crown and also that the Church on Sark was, in truth, a Church divided, the question arose of how to transfer the Living of Sark to the Crown.

Before this could be done however, an agreement, signed in 1823 by the then Seigneur and the Tenants, would need to be revoked.

The Agreement did three things:

Firstly, it attached the right of 36 pews to the respective Tenants as appurtenant to those Tenancies and made those Tenants liable to pay to the Seigneur rents at the rate of 5d per sitting per annum.

Secondly, these rents, together with an annual contribution of £1 from the Seigneur were supposed to go into a fund to provide for repairs, etc.

Thirdly, it placed the Tenants, on the one hand, and the Seigneur on the other under an obligation to provide, in equal shares, the cost of repairs in excess of the balance of the fund.

It would seem that not only had the pew rents not been paid, but no fund had been set up and, furthermore, the church fabric was badly dilapidated. Fortunately, even on Sark, a legal agreement has some binding force, and one of the luminaries of the Ecclesiastical Commission stated that whilst the agreement was certainly unusual, it was legally water-tight. However, providing all of the present Tenants and the current Seigneur agreed, the 1823 agreement could be revoked; nothing could be simpler.

Alas, the powers in London had reckoned without the "Sark

Factor". About sixty percent of the Tenants indicated their agreement to the revised terms. However, there was a small and obstinate minority who, it was said, would die in the last ditch rather than agree to any alteration. One Tenant is credibly reported to have said that if he were to give up his pew, he would lose his farm!

The Bishop now tried moral persuasion. Like the Biblical seed, this fell on stony ground. Mrs Hathaway (as she now was, having remarried) replied, *"As regards any moral liability, it should not be overlooked that the Seigneurs have always been very generous, having built the chancel and cemetery, given a house free (the vicarage), and I have paid the vicar's stipends for five years and now offer a valuable site and stone for a new vicarage."*

Two interesting points arise here. Firstly, La Dame had given the impression that she would provide the stone ready for use in building the new vicarage. She then said that what she really meant was "unquarried stone". At that time, unquarried stone was worth 6d per ton and estimating that it would need 350 tons to build a house, the value of Dame Sibyl's most generous gift was precisely £8.75p!

Secondly, now that she was remarried, she made the somewhat startling statement, *"I would be lacking in candour if I did not add that my husband,* **without whom, by island law, I cannot act,** *considers that in view of all of the foregoing gifts to the church, no moral discrepancies can be placed to my account."*

Dame Sibyl had more tricks in her bag. In July 1931, she wrote to the Bishop of Winchester stating that the Reverend Greenhow had informed her that not only was the vicarage in a bad state of repair, but also a certain staircase was actually in a dangerous condition. Her letter continued, *"In my father's letter of appointment of Mr. Greenhow no mention is made of repairs and thus I am not disposed to undertake these".* Considering that the vicar had five young children, this was not a particularly Christian position to adopt. She then informed the Bishop that according to her memory, he told her that the Reverend Greenhow would be transferred elsewhere within two years of 1928, a statement the Bishop denied making.

In January 1932, Greenhow left Sark to take up a living in Torteval, Guernsey, at which time Sark was without a minister of religion. Le Manoir was then sold. Although the living was advertised in the Church Times, no one would take it on without related accommodation. The island's pastoral needs were left to the Reverend Bestic who acted as locum. Whilst this sounds like a tame job, the Reverend Bestic was no fool and soon made his presence felt. He was so keen to serve Sark that he was prepared to subsidise his stipend out of his private means, and take lodgings until the matter was sorted out. His comments are illuminating.

He attended a meeting in January 1933 and reported as follows:

"La Dame presided. She is not a good chairman. She speaks very rapidly, incessantly and away from the point. The majority of the small farmers who are pew owners have the mentality of children. Mrs Hathaway read the Bishop's letter at express speed, and, obviously, they could not follow. The feudal instinct here is strong and though the Sarkese may differ with La Dame, they respect the position she occupies. The comments of the few present indicated that they thought that Mrs Hathaway was shirking her responsibilities. The withdrawal of the Manor House is the one point on which all of Sark is dead against her. Le Manoir has been used as the vicarage for 200 years. It has now been let."

Later in the same month, the matter came before Chief Pleas. The Reverend Bestic reports:

"Chief Pleas after discussion postponed the question of a grant of £500 to the Church until their next meeting. Mr Hathaway presided, La Dame being unwell. He is an American born (naturalised Briton) professes no religion, takes little interest in the affairs of the island and is unpopular. In fact, neither he nor Mrs Hathaway are often in Church. The item on the agenda which was supposed to be Mrs Hathaway's request for a grant of £500 appears simply to be 'To consider the question of a report on the Church of Sark.'"

The Reverend Bestic was of the opinion that the Hathaways

had little money. There is some evidence now to suggest that La Dame thought that Hathaway, being American was well-off, and he, knowing that Sibyl owned an island, thought she was well-off, when in fact, were it not a sad pun, they were both as poor as church mice. Or were they just mean of spirit as well as mean of purse?

The Church was not ready to consider taking legal action against La Dame and great minds were turned to the problem; Lawyers of the Guernsey Bar were consulted. These were clearly of the "two-handed" school of advocates for on the one hand, they opined that the Grant of 1565 to Helier de Carteret contained no obligation on the part of the Seigneur to provide for the spiritual needs of the Tenants nor could they find any authority which required the Lord of any Manor to provide for the spiritual ministrations of Tenants. On this point they were very wrong.

In olden times, the revenue of the incumbent of a parish church consisted of the tithes, variously also known as dismes or dîmes, one tenth of the produce of the land and adjoining sea. Such an incumbent was known as the Rector. In the case of Sark however, the tithes were granted to laymen, in this instance Helier de Carteret. These laymen became known as Lay Improprietors who received the tithes for their own account but **were bound,** as a consequence, to both nominate and pay the stipend of a curate to serve the parish. Thus when Dame Sibyl Hathaway tried to avoid paying the curate of Sark, she was quite wrong in her assertions that what she and past Seigneurs had done was merely an act of voluntary benevolence. She was in fact in breach of the 1565 Charter but sadly, the ecclesiastical lawyers never took this point on board.

However, on the other hand, they felt that the moral case was very strong in that for over 300 years successive Seigneurs had admitted a responsibility of sorts by providing a stipend and a dwelling house for the minister. After further consideration, legal action was dropped as an option.

In June 1933, the Reverend Bestic again reports to his Bishop:

139

"Mrs Hathaway's object is simply to free herself from financial obligation. She has no interest in the welfare of the Church. During the 14 months I have been here she has attended public worship fewer than six times and her policy has been obstructionist throughout. In her letter, Mrs Hathaway offers nothing of any value to herself and demands a great deal in return. She is cute, but not clever." Strong words indeed from a man of the cloth!

So strong was the feeling in Sark, that a Mr Mardon, father-in-law to Dr Pittard agreed that should any legal action be necessary to secure the rights of the Church of Sark, he would underwrite the expense. Since Mr Mardon was a member of the Wills Tobacco family, this was support of a very tangible kind.

In July 1933, things reached the proportions of a farce. La Dame threatened that if it was necessary to repair the Church, *"she would pull down the chancel which is her property and use the stones for that purpose."* Since the chancel was unconsecrated, much midnight oil was burnt by the Bishop's solicitor in London over this problem, with copious references to what happened at Arundel in Sussex, where a similar situation had occurred. The poor clerics could not recognise feminine temper when they saw it and quite overlooked the fact that the cost to her in tearing down the chancel and making good the rest of the church would be far in excess of the cost of the simple repairs. (Even today, the present Seigneur is said to have claimed that the ownership of the chancel is a bit of a grey area. Since cracks have recently appeared between the chancel and the church he would say that, wouldn't he? Fortunately, his grandmother's words are around to establish ownership, and thus place the consequent responsibility for repairs firmly upon him.)

In 1933, a new bishop, Bishop Cyril Garbett who later became Archbishop of York, wrote, "Sark has given me more correspondence than almost the whole of the rest of the Diocese". Dame Sibyl certainly knew how to provoke men of the cloth!

Then the Reverend Bastic resigned. Why he did so is not recorded, but just before then he reported to the Bishop that a lot of the church plate was in La Seigneurie when it ought to have been in the church. Even Mr Bestic withdrew from asking La Dame a direct question about this, and asked, instead, that the Bishop send him an official request to list Sark Church Plate which he could show to her as the reason for asking the question.

The Home Office received an anonymous letter purporting to come from outside Sark, but which probably originated from the Waller family, artist residents of Sark. A petition was even sent to the King. Sarkese are very adept at petitions and this one was from "Visitors to Sark", although the guiding hand of a resident can be clearly seen. It takes a very special kind of visitor to have knowledge of resolutions passed by Chief Pleas in an extraordinary meeting!

What enraged the petitioners was the agreement by Chief Pleas to divert £500 from the landing tax to build a house for the Minister of the Anglican Church on Sark to replace the one taken back by La Dame. This they held was ultra vires. They pointed out that in the Deed of Sale of Sark between Peter Carey le Pelley and Dame Marie Allaire, a paragraph existed which required the purchaser to pay the salary and provide a house for the minister. This Seigneurial obligation, they maintained, could not be shifted onto the island's budget.

Like most Sark petitions, it was a "cooked-up" job, inexpertly drafted but very transparent as to its real purpose. Also like most Sark petitions it seems to have withered on the vine.

Today, St Peter's Church on Sark is still owned by three persons/organisations. The clock tower belongs to the island of Sark, the chancel, added by the first Seigneur Collings in 1870, belongs to the Seigneur and the nave belongs to the church authorities. In this respect it may well be unique.

Between 1926 and 1938, Sark had no fewer than five clergymen moving the Dean of Guernsey, when conducting the frequent induction services, to utter the pious but unfulfilled wish that he hoped he would not have to do this again for many more years ahead. It was not to be, for between 1938 and 1956 Sark had a further four vicars, which, if one excludes the five years of Occupation, averaged one vicar every 30 months over the entire period from 1926 to 1956!

Since the Church is not generally renowned for rapid staff turnover and since the patronage of Sark was with the Seigneur, one does not need to be clairvoyant to determine where the blame lay.

CHAPTER THIRTY

THE GUNS OF SARK

Cannon at La Coupée, Sark, dating from around 1790

There are, dotted around Sark, eight cannon of the Napoleonic era. Assumed to have been sent from Guernsey, no record exists of their arrival and deployment. The gun illustrated above weighs just over 30 cwt and to transport, unload and move such guns around to some fairly remote locations must have been a Herculean task, yet it has gone unrecorded.

Barracks were built on Little Sark to house English troops but some of their guns would have been several miles from the base, on difficult terrain. Did they keep local stores of powder and shot near each gun? Could the gunners race to the gun site faster than enemy ships could transit the coast of Sark? Which had the tactical advantage, a gun 300 ft on a cliff firing down onto a small target, or a ship which, if it could get in the lee of the cliff, would be untouchable? Unfortunately, Sark was never really put to the test and these questions will remain unanswered.

The fact that the cannon were abandoned and remain on Sark to this day is due to new processes discovered in the early 19th century, to make flawless steel which could be drilled and shaped. Overnight, cast-iron armaments became obsolete and not worth the cost of collecting. Some attempt has been made to refurbish these guns and make new carriages for them and it is hoped this process will continue as they represent a tangible part of the island's past.

Apart from the cannon at La Coupée, most of the other guns are difficult to locate and are probably never seen by any visitors other than those who stay for a week or so. This is a great pity and consideration might be given to re-siting some of the more distant cannon to a purpose-built location near Harbour Hill where all visitors can share in Sark's history.

There are other cannon on Sark. At the Seigneurie, as well as the notorious cannon of 1572, there are several other 18th century guns said by the present Seigneur as having come from the privateer of Jean Allaire. This seems most unlikely. In addition there is an item from both World Wars, one a mortar and the other a German field gun left behind in 1945.

There is only one recorded instance of the guns of Sark being fired in anger. Around 1590 some English pirates had stolen from Brecqhou three cows belonging to some Guernseymen, and whilst sailing along the coast of Sark they fell in with a Sark boat returning from Guernsey. This they boarded, seizing one John Hotton, stealing a barrel of beer and removing a decorative pin from the person of Janette du Val. They were then challenged from the cliffs of Sark by Thomas Roo, the Sark Trumpeter of the Guard, who caused a cannon to be fired at the boat. This had the desired effect of driving off the pirates.

CHAPTER THIRTY-ONE

FISHERMEN'S TALES

Creux Harbour around 1900

Looked at from the sea it will be seen that Sark is not an easy island from which to fish. The cliffs tower up all around, some about 300 ft high. In fact there are only five practicable landings - in winter those with an on-shore wind are out of use. Around the island are rocks, some above the sea, some below, and when a sea is running there is a nasty overfall from these rocks, a sort of subterranean waterfall which can capsize a small boat. On a calm day, after a wind from the south-west, the long Atlantic swell sweeps in to dash itself against Little Sark, sometimes with a noise like a battleship firing its big guns. The daily spring tidal variation at Guernsey is as much as 10 metres and the tidal current runs at speeds between 8 to 10 knots. Even in calmer weather, boating is not for the inexperienced.

Boats seldom put to sea in rough weather. This is defined as when the salt of the spray can be tasted on the cliff tops! Until about 1920, no winter fishing was done at all but from then onwards boats went out after whiting. Of course, in those days boats were propelled by oars or sails for there were no mechanical means of propulsion.

On 6th October 1920, a measure was passed in Chief Pleas whereby a landing tax of one shilling per visitor was to be levied, the proceeds of which were to be expended on roads, harbours, La Coupée and other public works. This was too much for fishermen of Sark to bear and in November 1920, a petition was sent to King George V highlighting the following points:

(1)   The present insecurity of the harbour precludes fishing in the winter because the boats have to be hauled up.

(2)   That as all land in Sark is private, the term "public works" is minimal.

(3)   That as the franchise of Sark is entirely based on 40 Tenants, we are unrepresented in court.

(4)   The harbour is in a state of disrepair and all attempts to obtain repairs etc. have been blocked by Chief Pleas.

(5)   As the tax is being levied on those who land at Sark with great inconvenience, it is only just that the proceeds of such a tax should be used to make their arrival and departure easier.

(6)   All of the tax should be expended on the harbour.

The Home Office made the observation that this appears to have been the first time that a definite complaint of non-representation in Sark had been received. The petition was signed by 41 Sarkese, amongst whom were listed 10 Hamons, 8 Carrés, 6 Guilles, 3 Le Fèvres and 3 Viberts. Not for nothing was Sark known as "an island of cousins"!

In January 1921, The Government Secretary, one Colonel Macartney, was sent over by the Lieutenant Governor to see what was up. At the time, the Sark correspondent of the Guernsey Weekly Press wrote under the nom de plume of "Alert" and took the opportunity to keep the pot boiling by writing in his article the following:

"First of all we should like the Chief Plaids to be held in French, not in English so that the Tenants, most Sark men, may join in the discussion and know what they are asked to vote for without having recourse to an interpreter. Secondly, everyone, whether Tenant or not, should be represented; the fishermen who form a large percentage of the population have no vote. The Chief Plaids is held in English, with the result that the Tenants who do not understand the language do not vote. The laws are passed by half a dozen people who know practically nothing about the laws and customs of Sark and only study their own interests."

Although the fishermen got their representation in Chief Pleas in 1922, they had to wait many more years for their new harbour.

From about 1922, the octopus became very plentiful, indeed much too plentiful to the extent that in or around 1935, they arrived in Sark by the thousand; some of them were eight feet across. The first sign of this was that fishermen were catching many more lobsters as these were retreating ahead of the octopus.

Then the octopus were soon invading the lobster pots; sometimes up to eight would be found inside the pot. Difficult to remove, it was sometimes necessary to throw away a valuable pot. They fasten on to the lobster, sucking it clean. Octopuses have a kind of hood on their heads and the trick is to grab this and turn it inside out. This would, it seems, kill the creature.

During the 1930's a trawler was reported to have got a trawl full of octopuses off Brecqhou and when they pulled the trawl to the underside of the boat, the creatures attached themselves to the hull with their suckers. The skipper was lucky to be able to beach his vessel near Porte de Jument and free his trawl. Conger eels followed the octopuses and ate them, but in the late thirties, starfish were reported as being a problem.

Conger eels of the very largest size and weight abound in the Channel Islands probably because the sea bed presents so many rocky crevices where the creatures can grow undisturbed.

Ormers were another major source of food. Similar to but larger than an oyster, the ormer clung to rocks and had to be removed with some force at low tide. Generally four to six inches long with an oval shell - an iron hook is needed to remove them. Beaten with a wooden mallet to soften it, the ormer is then fried for about five to ten minutes until brown. Gourmets sing praises over this succulent dish. Ormers are now largely extinct through over-fishing, but rumour has it that a conservation group have located a small but thriving colony, the whereabouts of which they have sensibly decided to withhold.

Fishing from Sark, apart from perhaps three commercial fishermen, is now reduced to hobby fishing as the Sarkese have found easier ways of earning a living and, in common with much of the UK and Europe, fish stocks have become depleted. Nevertheless, what is landed is extremely clean and tasty.

OLD SARK RECIPE

La Soupe de Congre

Select a nice fresh conger eel about 7lbs in weight.
Cut the head off behind the gills.
Cut the tail off.
(Leave the middle portion to be stuffed and baked.)
With the head and tail add a quarter pound
of salted pork.
Add two carrots, four potatoes and four pints of water.
Bring to the boil and simmer for 30 minutes.
Strain it.
To the soup add a nice white cabbage,
half a pint of green peas,
four sprigs of parsley and two sprigs of thyme.
Add also two onions and five petals of marigold.
These must all boil gently for twenty minutes.
When the vegetables are soft
add half a pint of milk,
some butter and salt and pepper to taste.
Bring to the boil again,
and Enjoy!

CHAPTER THIRTY-TWO

SHIPWRECKED

Not surprisingly, Sark has been the scene of many shipwrecks although details of the majority of strandings have been lost over the years. In an age when a shipwreck was nothing out of the ordinary, nobody bothered to permanently record the mishap unless the circumstances were especially dramatic or the ship and cargo very valuable.

The earliest known record is of several French vessels, perhaps three in number, coming to grief on La Givaude off Brecqhou around 800 AD. In 1779, the East Indiaman *Valentine* struck La Neste, also off Brecqhou. This shipwreck is more fully described in another chapter.

In 1841 an American barque, *Sherwood* was sighted off Sark on its beam ends and in 1862, the French cutter *Alcyone* was wrecked on the northeast coast of the island. The following year, another French ship, the Chasse-Marée *Twelve Apostles* went down off Havre Gosselin and in 1885, a third French ship, *Charles* was wrecked at Grune au Nord.

The Brigantine *Joseph and Margaret* vanished near the Blanchard Rocks in 1887. These rocks lie to the east of Sark and are now marked with a buoy and light. In 1888, the sloop *Holbeach* of Boston, Lincs. was wrecked off Sark.

A wreck yet to be authenticated is that of the schooner *Agenoria* of Chester which was stranded near Platte Rock (off Port du Moulin on the west coast of Sark). This happened in May 1913. Four years later a steamer, *Hirondelle* of St Brieuc was wrecked off the island.

The next major wreck had overtones of comic opera. In March 1918 the French Vessel *Jeanne Marie*, of some 3,000 GRT struck a mine and sank in 160 feet of water. She was carrying a heavy cargo of copper ore which no doubt explained her rapid descent to the depths. This cargo was considered valuable enough to initiate a salvage operation by the Italian vessel, *Raffio*. In May 1931 the crew of the *Raffio* were attempting to lower a concrete block weighing some 8 tons over the side to act as a positional anchor.

A rope attached to the boom to prevent rapid outward movement snapped, causing the boom and the weight to move outboard at dangerous speed. The resultant shift of weight and momentum caused the *Raffio* to capsize. One must assume that the two wrecks lie close together, if not one on top of the other. It is not known whether any ore was ever recovered. Happily most of the crew escaped, there being but one casualty.

In 1922 a British steamer, *Cairnside* was wrecked south of Sark and on 22nd November 1932 a French ketch, *Le Poilu* went down off the Sark lighthouse.

A couple of miles west of Sark lies what is thought to be a tug with two barges. First located in 1969, nothing seems to be known of this wreck, which is odd, for it is unlikely to be very old and one would have thought that some enquiry would have been made when the tug and tow failed to turn up. It is of course quite possible that this was a German loss dating from the Occupation for which records have not survived.

The majority of stranded vessels were relatively small and unimportant, engaged in inter-island trade. Some were colliers carrying coal from Wales to France by the most direct route. Vessels like those in the convoy which contained the ill-fated *Valentine* were of an era when ships tried to stay in sight of land for navigational purposes.

Wrecks around Sark generally yielded rich booty for the islanders and it was not unknown for the bays to be so full of timber that it would have been possible to walk from one side to the other without wetting the feet.

There is a Sark law which prohibits the gathering of seagulls' eggs. This law is said to have its origins from pressure from local fishermen who held that if you could hear the cry of nesting birds you were almost on the rocks.

CHAPTER THIRTY-THREE

SARK VIEWED FROM GUERNSEY

In 1921, the Lieutenant Governor of Guernsey instructed a Colonel McCartney to visit Sark and prepare a report on how he viewed the island. These are his impressions.

Chief Pleas

Legislation can only be initiated by one of the Tenants. There is no quorum and no rules of debate. Proceedings are held in English which very few of the Tenants understand well, so most of them take little interest in the proceedings. Average attendance 11.

Justice

The only court is the Seneschal's. He sits as a judge being assisted by the Prévot and the Greffier. Judgements are not given in writing but are entered in a journal in French by the Greffier and signed by the Seneschal from time to time. Fines, including payments in lieu of "corvée", are levied by the Court. No account is kept of these and they are presumably annexed as perquisites by the officials. Licences of public houses, hotels etc. are granted by the Seigneur and regulated by Chief Pleas. Annual receipts of about £60 are paid to the Constable but there are no accounts for it and no information as to what is done with it.

Education
Nominally, education is compulsory but as no notice is taken of reports of non-attendance, in reality it is not. The boys' school should have 34 scholars, the girls' school 22 scholars. The standard of education is very low and the attendance very bad. The salaries of both the Schoolmaster and the Schoolmistress are quite inadequate. The Schoolmaster is only paid £50 per year and spends most of his time farming.

Fishermen
The fishermen pay no direct taxes and have no vote. They take practically all the fish to Guernsey as they demand a higher price than the Sarkese can afford. They therefore do little for the benefit of the island wherein they live and keep their boats. The Sark Constitution provides that sufficient food must remain on the island before any is exported, but this is a "dead letter".

Agriculture
The soil is badly cultivated and very dirty. The farmers complain that they cannot get grain ground as the only mill, the Seigneur's, is out of order.

General situation
Apart from innkeepers who are very prosperous and some of the farmers and fishermen, the bulk of the people are badly clothed and their cottages are poor and dirty.

The Seigneur
In former years when Sark was more or less isolated and when the Seigneur was a man who did his duty, no doubt the ancient system of government would suffice. The character of the present Seigneur shows that it is not possible to rely upon the holder of the seigneurial rights always being a suitable person to hold the large powers for good or ill possessed by him under the present constitution. The Seigneur is not

unpopular though he commands no sort of respect. Many of the rights he exercises do not relate back to the 1565 Charter and no objection is seen to the Crown depriving him of them.

CHAPTER THIRTY-FOUR

SARK VIEWED FROM WHITEHALL

From about 1920, the files at the Home Office started to bulge with correspondence about Sark. These are some of the choicer items:

1921 May

The island is at present in a state of mild anarchy. There are no proper police arrangements. Among the natives themselves this leads to nothing more than a prevalence of petty theft, but in the summer when crowds of excursionists pour in, it might easily have more serious results. Education is in a very poor state and public works are generally neglected. This is due to negligence, not poverty.

1923 June

I spent a week at the Greffe on Sark and went through their records. I found the books much better-kept than I had expected. The trouble is that they have no index or abstract, so they have to look through all of the old records to find out what the law is on a particular subject. And, as it is the custom of Chief Pleas to pass a law in one year, then cancel or change it in a subsequent year, they then find that there already was an ancient law on the same subject and they revert to this. Then they forget what they have done and legislate "de novo". No-one knows what the laws are, with the consequence that not many of them are observed.

1923 July

The Seneschal is honestly trying to do his best, but he is hampered by the fact that he is the local doctor and does not want to put his clients' backs up. An instance has arisen over asking the Admiralty for expert assistance over the new harbour. Both the Seigneur and the Seneschal are very averse to asking for help without Chief Pleas' sanction. Chief Pleas would approve if the Seigneur approved, but he is very weak and a bit obstinate. Behind it all is the usual suspicion of "graft" and interest in who is going to get any fees, rather than the quality of the advice.

1923 July

I fear that we shall never get much done with the Seigneur. We have been reluctant to deprive him of any rights, but he is becoming impossible in that he won't do anything himself and strongly objects to anyone else doing anything.

1923 August

The Seigneur is a bit of a stumbling block and is now taking up the attitude of King Log and is following a policy of masterly inactivity.

Date Unknown

My present concern is to introduce some ideas on sanitation. I have got as far as setting up a Sanitation Authority with a committee which Chief Pleas agreed to, but in the next breath refused to give them any power to act. They argue that if a man owns a stream of water he has the perfect right to pollute it if he wishes to, regardless of his neighbours. The reading of their debates is like a comic opera.

1926 October

The Constitution is complete at present. It does not seem right to me that individuals who pay no rates or taxes should be allowed to

158

sit in Chief Pleas. However, Sark Chief Pleas would have provided matter for a Gilbert and Sullivan opera, and as the majority of members never open their mouths, there is no need to worry. The longer I live here the more I am convinced that Sark's chief desire is to be left alone. Any hint of anything new is at once regarded as interference. The people are really much the same as in 1565 when Helier de Carteret brought his 40 bandits from Jersey. They are in need of a sober doctor!

1927 August

There has never been a nurse in Sark, but Sark people will first have to realise that the present system, under which a woman about to become a mother relies on the assistance of her neighbour to act as midwife, is not the best. Also, they would never allow a nurse to be imported and this means getting a Sark girl sent to Guernsey to be trained.

1930 January

La Dame's marriage has been the only excitement here. Mr Hathaway is American-born but now a British subject. I made his acquaintance shortly after the marriage but was not greatly impressed - not the sort to go down well with the islanders.

1930 July

The Sark Chief Pleas recently passed an ordinance making vaccination compulsory, but with a conscientious objectors' clause! It has taken many years to get this measure through.

1936 September

A stone-crushing machine was recently imported into the island. It weighs about 2.5 tons and the Seigneur very wisely used his tractor to haul it up Harbour Hill as it would have been very difficult to have done so with horses. However, in using his tractor on the roads in this way, he unfortunately infringed a Sark Ordinance and the Gilbertian situation arose of the Seigneur having to appear before the Sark Court and being fined half a crown by his Seneschal.

CHAPTER THIRTY-FIVE

UP WITH THE LARK!

This is not the story of some splendid songbird indigenous to the island of Sark but of practices carried out on Sark under the cover of feudalism. Whenever man has levied taxes or placed onerous regulations upon his fellow-citizens, a proportion of those citizens have invariably sought ways to avoid compliance. As the world became more complex those taxpayers able to afford it have hired lawyers and accountants for advice on how to minimise their tax burden. As soon as fiscal authorities brought out new counter-measures, the lawyers responded with new methods of avoidance. One of these avoidance devices involves the island of Sark.

Sark has no income or corporation taxes, neither does it have any form of company law. Many jurisdictions which do have these "blessings", use a *"place of management and control"* test to determine whether or not a company registered in a particular jurisdiction, should also be taxed there. The ideal position to aim for is to be able to prove that a company is resident elsewhere than in the country of incorporation. If this second country levies no taxes, then great benefits are to be reaped. Sark was, and is, ideal. As well as having no taxes, it has no regulatory powers and, what is more important, it has a large number of residents willing to co-operate in misleading foreign jurisdictions. In short, those Sarkese are willing to tell lies for a nominal fee. Honour apparently comes cheaply in Sark, and for £150 per year, a Sarkese can always be found to act as a director.

To all intents the Sark Lark started when Jersey and Guernsey evolved into off-shore financial centres in the early 1970s. Both islands instituted a category of exempt company but these were still taxed in their island of incorporation even if the shareholders were non-resident and no trade was conducted within the islands. The way around this was to change the place of management and control to Sark which levied no Corporation Tax.

However, in reality, the idea started much earlier. In 1919 William A Toplis, the noted Sark artist assisted in the purchase of shares in Stocks Hotel by some wealthy Englishmen. Wondering why those shareholders then made so many visits to inspect what must have been a very small investment, arrived at the following conclusion:

"Sark could become a haven for those who wished to conduct business in a manner which might be considered unacceptable, or even illegal, in England. With no official company law in Sark, the owners of Sark companies would be free from prosecution anywhere in the world for any acts committed in the world, providing only that the orders appeared to come from Sark. Therefore if a Sark resident could be persuaded to "front" a business, any amount of evil could be perpetrated throughout the world with complete immunity and vast profit. Sark which had been populated in order to prevent sixteenth century piracy, would become a seething den for inflicting on the world, the effects of twentieth century's far worse economic piracy."

When one considers the harassment which Sark meted out to Toplis, he truly was a prophet without honour in his own land.

Thus began the heyday of the Sark lark. The first tangible evidence may have been the introduction into Sark in 1965 of a postal franking machine, for use by "Who's Who of British Engineers". A second one arrived in October 1969, used by Euro-Books Ltd. Whilst it is not absolutely certain these organisations were under the Sark Lark, it would be unusual for an island the size of Sark to have need of franking machines for normal volumes of correspondence.

In those days, board meetings had to be physically held on Sark and the practice grew of appointing non-residents of the Channel Islands as directors whose job it was to go to Sark to hold meetings. Tales are told of groups of sea-sick men in dark suits, being hauled up Harbour Hill by tractor to hold a few dozen board meetings, and to partake of a few medicinal brandies, at the Bel-Air Hotel. If the boat timetables did not permit the climb up to the hotel, meetings were held on the quayside with the party returning on the same boat.

On one occasion, fog in the Channel prevented all boat traffic, so an aeroplane was hired to circle over Sark airspace whilst the formal business was concluded. A certificate was obtained from the pilot, duly confirming that at the times of each meeting, the plane was indeed over Sark!

It did not take long for someone to realise that if they appointed Sarkese as directors, not only would the need for travelling around the islands be dispensed with, it would be possible to so structure the company that the two Sark residents could, by themselves, conduct a quorate board meeting. In practice, this means their simply signing a piece of paper and popping it back in the post.

In 1989 both Jersey and Guernsey changed their laws, effectively doing away with the need for Sark directors. However, as the saying goes, *"as one door closes, another opens"* and Sark was perceived to have a much more universal advantage. Indeed, the "golden years" of the Sark Lark then began in earnest. Nowadays, Sarkese are directors of companies in the Isle of Man, the Republic of Ireland, the United Kingdom, Hong Kong, Panama, Liechtenstein, Luxembourg, The Bahamas, British Virgin islands, the Netherlands Antilles and Switzerland. This list is far from complete.

The rationale has also expanded. Evasion of tax is undoubtedly the prime motive, but there are now other reasons to involve Sark. Illegalities of all kinds occasionally come to light involving Sark-directed companies. Gun running, pornographic distributors and financial scams of various hues have all surfaced. The mechanics are simple, as is demonstrated by this case history.

Persons decide that they are going to engage in an illegal or anti-social activity. They first visit a company formation agent in, say, the Isle of Man and acquire an "off-the-shelf company". Of course they do not state why they want the company, but its Memorandum and Articles will be sufficiently wide to permit any activity to be carried out. They then obtain, normally from quite respectable lawyers and accountants in Guernsey or Jersey, the names of two Sark residents who are prepared to act as directors. These Sarkese then execute a statutory Declaration of Non-Residency in the Isle of Man. The only subsequent requirement of the Manx authorities is that a company return be submitted every year giving the names of directors and enclosing a cheque for just over £700 to meet Manx treasury fees.

The company has now vanished as far as the Manx regulators are concerned. There are no regulatory authorities in Sark. No-one, anywhere, sees the accounts. No-one anywhere, regulates the company. When, as occasionally happens, the company is exposed, the only two names which appear are those of the two Sarkese. These then resign and protest vigorously with wailings of, *"we didna ken, we didna ken"*.

Of course, these two Sarkese have no access to company assets and indeed, they are required to sign undated letters of resignation upon appointment. For their services, they receive fees of between £150 and £280 per year, which may sound a small sum of money until it is realised that some individual Sarkese have nearly 3,000 such directorships.

It has been calculated that Sarkese hold between them, somewhere between 15,000 and 24,000 directorships which, at the minimum of £150 each, brings into their collective pockets between £2,250,000 and £3,600,00 per year. Not all Sarkese are involved by any means. The hard core numbers about one hundred persons out of some 500 but unfortunately, their activities malign the honest hard-working majority.

Apart from any limited amounts subsequently spent locally, on home improvements for example, none of this money benefits the island of Sark.

Lest it be thought that income from the Sark Lark, and indeed, as was recently hinted in the press, also the Seigneur's Treizième, finds its way into their island coffers, examination of the following extract from the *1996 Accounts of the Island of Sark* will clearly debunk that idea.

ISLAND OF SARK
REVENUE ACCOUNT FOR THE YEAR ENDED
31ST DECEMBER 1996

	Year ended 31.12.96 £
REVENUE	
Impot (Duties on Imports)	195,760
Agricultural levies, etc.	1,903
Poll tax	68,518
Harbour dues	15,964
Investment income (Interest)	21,996
Crane receipts	30,971
Miscellaneous income	22,556
	357,668
EXPENDITURE	
Salaries and wages	89,373
Repairs and maintenance	13,271
Grants, subsides, etc.	14,315
Education	34,562
Harbours	29,493
Crane expenses	19,199
Police services, etc.	3.699
Miscellaneous expenditure	53,054
	256,966
SURPLUS FOR THE FINANCIAL YEAR	£ 100,702

There is virtually no "trickle down" effect other than a plethora of home extensions and garden sheds to house the fax machines and the filing cabinets. A joke on Sark is the spoof headline, "Sark shed burns down, 500 persons homeless"

Members of Chief Pleas are involved, indeed approximately one quarter of that august body are listed as company directors in the registries of the world. One lady advertises extensively on the inter-net and unashamedly proclaims her connections with Sark's Parliament of which she is a Member. The Seigneur and his wife seemed to have specialised in the Panama market where they have been given grand titles such as El Presidente (The President) and La Tesora (The Treasurer). Whether either of these persons has actually ever been to Panama City, other than during a world cruise, is open to question! What the fascination of Panama is, of course, anyone's guess. It might be a coincidence that it is geographically situated between Colombia and Nicaragua, two countries with a certain reputation in the hard drug industry. On the other hand, it might all revolve around coffee. Whatever the reason, the Panamanian Government was sufficiently concerned to despatch an envoy to Sark recently.

Another fascinating directorship, held by Mrs Beaumont is, or was, in a UK Company where the shareholders include Cantrade Beitleguns AG, H Schaefer and Abdullah Al Saud, all of Switzerland. Why these foreign luminaries required the services of a modest housewife from a backwater like Sark is not known.

These Sarkese neither know, nor care, what "their" companies do, being quite content to sit back and see the cheques roll in as a reward for telling lies, for this is what it amounts to. They make legal statements to the effect that "X" Ltd is managed and controlled in Sark, when this is patently not the case. They seem to be totally unaware, or if aware, totally indifferent, to the fact that they are small but key links in a chain which enables all sorts of illegalities to flourish and remain undetectable.

In 1998, the US Narcotics Bureau reported that it was investigating a drug-related money-laundering operation involving companies in Guernsey, the Isle of Man and the Republic of Ireland, all of which had Sarkese as directors.

More recently, a Scandinavian unit trust was milked of many millions and at the end of the long trail involving companies in Monte Carlo are two residents of Sark, indeed, they are the two at the top of the Sark Lark league.

A document has come into the author's hands purporting to have been issued in 1994 by The International Tourist Club (Sark) located at Jardin Louise Sark. This offers, to persons who need never set foot on Sark, some quite attractive services. In fact, so detailed are the services offered, one wonders if the so-called "bulletin" is a hoax. It would seem that ITC (Sark) can provide the following:

- A Sark Driving Licence
- Bank accounts at Sark banks
- A spurious lease of Sark property
- A Sark telephone number
- Affidavits to the Guernsey Passport Office evidencing five years "residence" in Sark
- Laundry services (of money!)
- Residence permits for Great Britain

ITC (Sark) states that the Seigneur, Law Officers and Parliament are in the Club's "pocket" and on the club payroll in one form or another. Hoax or not, ITC has advertised its existence in the Financial Times and glossy magazines which is a fairly expensive way of perpetrating a practical joke.

One does not need to be qualified or experienced in company management. Retired naval officers, art dealers, hoteliers, farmers, confectioners and fishemen are all grist to the Sark Lark mill. Indeed, one of the finest exponents of the Sark Lark originally came to the island as a collector of pig swill from the local hotels and held distinctly left-wing views.

Defenders of the Sark Lark often state that whilst admittedly, they do not know what their companies do, how can anyone else then say that those companies might be engaged in unlawful acts? To answer this, one has to point out that firstly, people do not hand out money to perfect strangers without good cause and secondly, if there is nothing to hide, why bother to hide it? When one can occasionally pierce the veil of obscuration, one can determine by the way the company has been set up, that it must hide an illegality of one sort or another.

These participants in the Sark Lark also state that Sark is facilitating international trade and should be left alone to provide this valuable service. To support the contention, they have formed an organisation to regulate these directorships. Such statements and reactions have to be taken with a very large pinch of salt! As far as can be ascertained, the only requirement this new organisation lays upon the shoulder of the "Sark Larkists" is to return the number of non-resident directorships they hold.

A great oddity on Sark is the existence of branches of two major clearing banks. There are few villages of 600 souls in the UK which can match this level of banking coverage. Banks have long ceased to provide a social service and if a branch is seen to be uneconomic, it is promptly shut. Of course, great inconvenience would accrue to Sark if it had no bank whatsoever but customer convenience has never been high in the minds of those in the banking parlours of the City of London.

To be fair to Sark, there is much concern over the Sark Lark. So much so that in 1992, it is said, a draft law was sent from

Sark to Guernsey in an attempt to legislate to stop it. Guernsey apparently was so taken with the law that it decided to adopt it for itself and has never returned it. As a result, a law, allegedly drafted in 1992, is nowhere near the Sark statute book as we approach the new millennium.

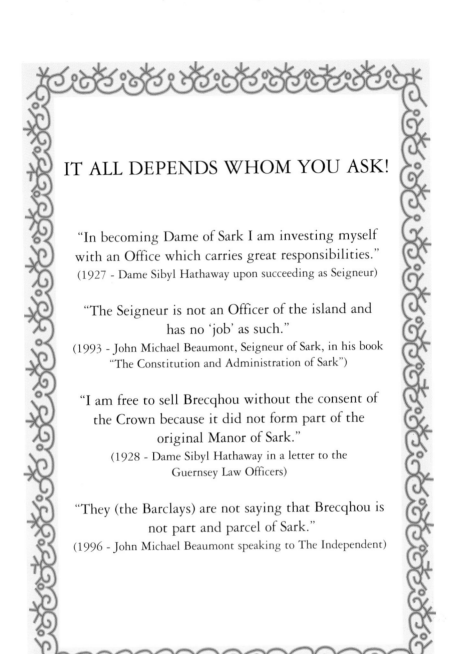

IT ALL DEPENDS WHOM YOU ASK!

"In becoming Dame of Sark I am investing myself with an Office which carries great responsibilities."
(1927 - Dame Sibyl Hathaway upon succeeding as Seigneur)

"The Seigneur is not an Officer of the island and has no 'job' as such."
(1993 - John Michael Beaumont, Seigneur of Sark, in his book "The Constitution and Administration of Sark")

"I am free to sell Brecqhou without the consent of the Crown because it did not form part of the original Manor of Sark."
(1928 - Dame Sibyl Hathaway in a letter to the Guernsey Law Officers)

"They (the Barclays) are not saying that Brecqhou is not part and parcel of Sark."
(1996 - John Michael Beaumont speaking to The Independent)

CHAPTER THIRTY-SIX

NEVER MIND THE EVIDENCE

LET'S HAVE THE SENTENCE!

The Prison on Sark

Helier de Carteret had, under the Charter of 1565, the right to hold a Sark Court. This he did in 1579 but made it subordinate to the Jersey Court and Jersey law, which upset the authorities in Guernsey. In 1582 the Guernsey Bailiff crossed over to Sark, called for a muster of the Quarantaine, and finding it to be short of the required 40 eventually seized the Court records and declared Sark forfeit to the Crown.

This was a trifle unfair because nothing in the 1565 Charter required de Carteret to do anything other than cause Sark to be inhabited by at least forty men. Parading those forty men on demand was not a requirement of the Charter. It was eventually sorted out by an Order in Council of 1583 which appointed the Sark Court to be legally subordinate to the Guernsey Court.

In 1675 a second Order in Council was obtained which abolished the 1583 court and substituted in its place the court as it exists today. The composition of the court consists of a Seneschal (Judge) appointed by the Seigneur. He is assisted by a Prévot (Sheriff) and a Greffier (Clerk of the Court) also appointed by the Seigneur. Since the Seigneur approves the appointment of the Constable and Vingtenier (assistant Constable) this makes for a rather interesting situation. There cannot be many places in western Europe where one man appoints the entire judiciary and approves (or not, as the whim take him), the appointment of the entire police force without any popular mandate and answerable to no-one.

Indeed, on Sark, you can be arrested by the Seigneur's man, brought to court by the Seigneur's man, judged by the Seigneur's man and if found guilty, be escorted off the island by the Seigneur's man. It is hard to escape the conclusion that if someone fell foul of the Seigneur, any Seigneur, their life could be made very difficult indeed. When it is considered that the Seigneur is also Chairman of the Planning Committee and can prevent someone from buying a property on the island by refusing grant of congé, this is a level of power far more in keeping with a banana republic. In addition, the Seigneur is a member of the Douzaine, the island's executive. Just in case there are any loose ends which might allow a legal loophole to be found, the most recent reference book on the Constitution of Sark has been written by the present Seigneur.

Sark has been described as fascist and whilst at first sight, this may appear to be a harsh judgement, compare Sark with fascist Spain under Franco. The Head of State was Franco. He appointed the Executive. The Cortes (Parliament) which met two or three times a year, when the President so decided, passed laws which Franco did, or did not accept. The president of the Cortes was appointed by Franco. So there are many similarities.

The actual machinery of law and order is implemented by a Constable and a Vingtenier. The constable holds the office for a year, when he is succeeded by the Vingtenier. Until 1949, these officials were unpaid, but in an unrecorded decision of Chief Pleas, it was decided that the officials could help themselves to monies held in the Hotel and Public House licence fees' account and pay themselves whatever they thought to be appropriate. Since, until the late fifties, these accounts were not public knowledge, a certain amount of licence was taken over the quantum of payments. Neither of these officials is trained in the maintenance of law and order.

Whilst most of the business dealt with by the Sark Court is fairly petty and humdrum, because in spite of its delusions of grandeur, it is merely a "Court of First Instance"; there were some interesting cases in the 17th century over the question of samphire.

Samphire, or perchepierre, also known as St Peter's herb, grew in abundance on Sark and Brecqhou and was highly prized. Indeed, it was so highly prized that theft of samphire was not unknown and cases were heard in the Sark Court. At one stage, in 1604, the Seigneur tried to claim right of samphire on Sark, but was defeated in Court by Messrs Raulin Vaudin, François Vibard and Mathew Alexandre. Samphire was not supposed to be cut before the month of June, possibly as a conservation measure, but the Court records are full of cases where persons could not resist "jumping the gun", so much so that around 1620 the ordinance regarding the June date was repealed.

The Court did give serious consideration to the samphire cases. In 1611 a rather involved case which on the face of it looked proven beyond any reasonable doubt, was dismissed with the thoughtful words:

"The Court having fully considered the testimony of the witnesses finds that however much that it saw considerable appearance that the ordinance had been breached by the defendant nevertheless does not find that it is sufficiently convinced."

There does not appear to be any ready reference book to the entire laws of Sark. For example, in 1913, mention was made of an Ordinance forbidding people to collect outside the public places of worship whilst divine service was taking place. Apparently a number of Sarkese were in the habit of congregating outside the church to talk and smoke. Like most of Sark's laws this was never enforced. It must be assumed that an over-zealous constable could catch out an unwary group of holidaymakers even in the 21st century.

Another interesting insight to the Sark of the 1920's is the following report from the Guernsey Weekly Press:

"Burglary, housebreaking, stealing of goods on the quay, stealing of crops and breaking down of gates go on night after night. If one complains to the Seneschal he sends you on to the Constable. The latter refuses to move unless you give him the name of the thief! There is a gang of them; soon it will be dangerous to walk the roads at night."

They were more confused in 1945. Towards the end of March in that year, i.e. before the war had ended, Seneschal William Carré's son was given a tree by the German Commandant of Sark to share among various residents of Sark for use as fuel. Assuming the version of events to be true, then Mr Carré's son came by the tree legitimately he having the approval of an accredited representative of the occupying power.

On 9th June 1945, less than one month after Sark was liberated when all should have been sweetness and light, William Carré (the father, **not** the son) was charged before the Sark Court as having, *"stolen, cut, broken, uprooted or otherwise destroyed a tree belonging to the owner of Le Manoir."* He was found guilty of having *"taken possession of the tree,"* a finding which bore little relation to the charge without regard to the fact that it was his son who first obtained the offending item.

He was fined £1 which on appeal to the Royal Court of Guernsey was quashed. He was not re-established as Seneschal in spite of the fact that upon appeal he was found to be innocent.

The Sark gaol is often quoted in conjunction with the charming case of the girl who stole a handkerchief and was "locked up" with the door left open because she was afraid. How utterly quaint - how utterly Sark! What is less well-known is the case where an English resident, known to be mentally deficient, was lodged in the prison because he entered the house of the schoolmaster and refused to leave. Quite docile, rather confused, but of otherwise unblemished character, this poor unfortunate wretch was thrown overnight into the Sark gaol.

The prison was damp. The roof, constructed of bricks, much in the style of a lime kiln, is porous. There are no damp courses and the walls are often also damp. The two cells measure about 9ft by 5ft. There is a corridor running the length of the establishment, measuring some 20ft by 4ft in which a fireplace has been constructed as part of the original building of 1856. The fireplace was unserviceable. At the end of the corridor is an open cesspit to serve as a toilet. Of toilet paper there was none, neither was there running water, except of course, through the roof. With no lights other than what natural light enters via two portholes, the Sark Gaol is certainly no health farm. Into this "Black Hole of Calcutta" was thrust the "criminal" to ponder his misdemeanor throughout the long night.

At 8.45 the following morning the whole panoply of the Sark Court arrived. Imagine the scene, a sick man, prostrate on a camp bed, quite unfit to plead, without legal representation or legal aid. Around him stood the panjandrums of the Sark Judiciary. Justice must not only be done, but must be seen to have been done.

A far cry indeed from the little girl and the handkerchief. There are no Crown Officers on Sark, no lawyers, no-one for a poor unfortunate to turn to. This would not happen today. Well, possibly not, but the example just quoted took place in 1958 which is only forty odd years ago, so who can say?

So, how effective is the judicial system on Sark? Two recent pieces of legislation are considered here.

The Fishing (Sark) Ordinance 1996 set out with the quite well-intentioned motive of protecting the waters around Sark from over-fishing. Nobody could complain about that. However, the area of exclusion zone forms a box which surrounds Sark and Brecqhou. This is described as Sark's territorial waters. Any person brought to the Court under this ordinance would escape quite easily because Sark has no territorial waters. Sark is not a "territory". Additionally, the jurisdiction of the Sark Court stops at the low-water-mark. There is an additional qualification in that if a mounted man, up to his stirrups in the sea, can touch a wreck with his lance, that too falls under the jurisdiction of the Sark Court but for the purposes of this particular ordinance, anything beyond the foreshore is the responsibility of the owner, i.e. the Crown. A good advocate would soon have his client free if this ordinance were used to bring a prosecution.

The next piece of legislation is "The False Documents and Domicile, etc. (Bailiwick of Guernsey) law 1998. The origin of this borders upon farce.

There were at least four houses on Sark which were "home" to persons and organisations which were clearly located elsewhere. The major player operated from a modest house named "Caro Mio" which housed at one time or another, some 200 phantom residents. Exotic companies resided there, like the Software Factory and Charly Acquisitions as well as important executives, like Rudolf H Krebs who was so busy, he was never "at his desk at the moment". Nothing adverse has been detected from these residents in the way that certain Sark Lark activities have been found to be illegal, but Sark decided to dispense with this facility. It is the author's personal view that "Caro Mio" was thrown to the wolves to take the heat off the real Sark Lark.

Nevertheless, in early 1998, this activity was banned by law.

In a survey taken in September 1999, the author found that of a sample phantom residents of Caro Mio, 68% appeared to be still in business. A comparison shows that whilst a few phantoms have gone, a few new ones have appeared, which would indicate that it is "business as usual". Since to unplug a telephone line is the work of but a moment, the fact that so many lines are still operational points to a complete inability of Sark to enforce its own laws.

The author is of the personal opinion that the False Documents and Domicile Act could be applied to end the Sark Lark since there appears to be no difference between a person declaring that someone lives at "Caro Mio", when he clearly does not, and a person declaring that XYZ Inc. of Panama is managed and controlled from Sark when it clearly also is not.

Although the small Sark Court and its amateur officers are the stuff of fairy tales it is hard to see how accurate justice can be dispensed. The present Seneschal is an electrical engineer, doubtless of excellent skill. How can such a person act as a judge? As far as can be ascertained, he has no legal training and there is no advocate in the Court acting as clerk to discreetly advise the judge when he has overstepped the mark.

More seriously however, is the fact that virtually every miscreant is known to the judge. In the UK, the least a judge could do would be to declare this fact to the lawyers acting for both parties. He might even consider disqualifying himself to sit on the case. The last thing he would wish to do would be to have his decision unwittingly swayed by his personal knowledge of the defendant. If you "know" a man is a habitual poacher for example, and he comes up before you on a poaching charge, it would be most difficult not to mix personal knowledge with hard evidence.

The author has seen several references where Seneschals have volunteered to the Court that they know of certain relevant facts - therefore the evidence given by one of the parties to the dispute must be incorrect. This seems to be a rum sort of justice. This observation is not meant to be a reflection on the integrity of Seneschals but on the system which places them in office. Human nature being what it is, colouring the evidence with personal knowledge of the defendant is hard to avoid.

The time seems long overdue for preliminary justice on Sark to be dispensed not from a local-grown judge but from a qualified visiting member of the Guernsey Judiciary.

Finally and on a lighter note, Sark is probably the last remaining place where the "Clameur de Haro" is still valid. This is a form of instant injunction which requires anyone infringing the rights of another, to cease immediately when the person offended against executes the Clameur. To do this, the complainee must, in front of witnesses, and on his knees, recite the Lord's Prayer in French and then cry out "Haro, Haro, Haro, A mon aide mon Prince, on me fait tort". He must then hurry away to the Greffe office and register his Clameur and pay a deposit of money. The matter is then frozen until the Court hears the complaint. In an age where even remembering the entire Lord's Prayer in English is a dying art, let alone reciting it in French, the practical effectiveness of the Clameur must be receding.

CHAPTER THIRTY-SEVEN

OF THE PEOPLE, BY THE PEOPLE, FOR THE PEOPLE

Government is exercised through Chief Pleas, over which the Seneschal presides. For centuries Chief Pleas consisted of the head of the household of the forty original Tenements. Whilst this may have been acceptable in the sixteenth and seventeenth centuries, discontent was never far below the surface and sometimes on the surface.

For example, in 1892, Sark was in a ferment because a recent law passed by Chief Pleas gave Tenants the right to shoot rabbits the whole year round, but ordaining sundry close times for the remaining inhabitants. This was considered unjust by the non-Tenants who showed their displeasure by burning down a stable and barn owned by Thomas de Carteret and a cart shed owned by Elie Guille at Carrefour. In spite of the Seneschal and the two constables being described as "on the alert", no traces of the perpetrators were discovered

An illuminating comment from 1897, by the Sark correspondent of the "Guernsey Moon and Visitors' Guide" (a forerunner of "The Guernsey Evening Press") is full of irony.

"The Committee appointed to carry out the festivities and rejoicing to commemorate the Diamond Jubilee have had a meeting this week in the boys' schoolroom. Five committeemen were present, all Tenants, in whom, it is well known, rests all the wit, wisdom, land and money of this gem of the sea. Their

superior position also proves them to be repositories of the erudition and knowledge of the island and there was no need for the schoolmaster who was absent from the counsels; he is only the second son of a tennon and could not fit into the mortice. Like Jacob of old, he had no birthright but must obtain one by purchase, or go without."

From 1922 onwards, as a result of the Sark Reform Act 1922, twelve "Deputies of the People" were introduced on an elective basis. This originated from a petition from the fishermen who felt that they had no proper representation in Chief Pleas. The authorities in Guernsey seemed to favour change, and indeed sent quite a constructive plan to Sark, which Chief Pleas speedily over-ruled (See opposite).

Thus the various drafts of the 1922 Act were shuffled backward and forwards between London, Guernsey and Sark for consideration. Even whilst these drafts were being examined and argued about, Seigneur Collings and his Tenants were busy cooking up a counter-petition to defeat the proposed changes and keep to the old ways. This petition was submitted to the Home Office in January 1922. Some 243 persons were said to have signed but when one examines the original document, some curious anomalies leap out.

For example, it is painfully obvious from a comparison of the handwriting, that the heads of most families also signed for the other family members. Four members of the Remphrey family and five members of the Hamon family, in each case, had their "signatures" and addresses executed in identical handwriting and numerous husbands signed for their wives. No attempt was made to disguise this fact. Getting petitions to look genuine was never Sark's strong point, even today. Nevertheless, it took four elections before the requisite number of Deputies was appointed.

The action taken in 1922 might look like a move in the democratic direction, but overlooks the fact that there is always an inbuilt majority of persons (the unelected Tenants) who themselves,

Seigneur and Gentlemen Tenants of Sark.

HIS EXCELLENCY THE LIEUT.-GOVERNOR believes that the time has now come for a change in the government of the Island of Sark.

He wishes more or less to restore the ancient system which was in force in the time of Queen Elizabeth, with some modifications, and trusts that the Chief Pleas will consult as to whether they approve of the propositions before them :—

1. That the Chief Pleas still remain the only legislative body in Sark.

2. That a Seneschal be appointed by the Crown on the recommendation of the Lieut.-Governor, to sit, as in Alderney, as Judge and President of the Chief Pleas.

3. That the Chief Pleas consist of the Seneschal and seven Deputies elected for five years as follows :

   By the Seigneur   1
   ,,   Tenants   2
   ,,   Fishermen   2
   ,,   Farmers and others   2
   ————
   7

   All Deputies to be residents of Sark. During the first five years one Deputy to retire annually by lot, and all to be eligible for re-election.

4. That the Crown appoint an inhabitant of Sark recommended by the Lieut.-Governor as Prevost and Greffier (the offices being combined), and another as Treasurer.

5. Six Douzeniers shall be elected annually for one year by all the inhabitants, and be eligible for re-election. They will sit and debate in the Chief Pleas, but will not have a vote.

6. The Seneschal or his deputy must be present at all meetings of the Chief Pleas; also the Prevost. All meetings to be open to the public.

7. The sittings of the Chief Pleas to be held after Christmas, Easter, and St. Michael, but the Seneschal to have the power to call for a meeting at any time, with the consent of the Lieut.-Governor. The Seneschal to have a casting vote. The Seneschal or his deputy and four Deputies to form a quorum.

8. All Ordinances passed by the Chief Pleas to be registered by the Royal Court of Guernsey. If the Court refuses registration they will be nullified.

9. The Seigneur's veto to be abolished.

10. The Court of Justice to be composed as at present, of the Seneschal, with the same powers, except that in civil cases his powers will be limited.

11. The Court to grant licences for Inns and Publichouses, the fees to be credited to the General Revenue of the Island.

12. A Constable and Vingtenier to be elected by all the inhabitants.

13. The Seneschal, the Prevost, and the Treasurer to be paid from the Revenue controlled by the Crown.

14. The Sark Police to be under the control of the Inspector of the States Police in Guernsey.

15. All Strangers wishing to remain more than six weeks in Sark to obtain permission from the Seneschal, not from the Seigneur.

JOHN MACARTNEY,
Colonel, Secretary to the Government.

represent just 40 people of Sark. The remaining 500 or so inhabitants have to make do with the twelve elected Deputies permanently in a minority. Whilst Sark proclaims, with misguided reasoning that with 52 Members of Parliament to some 550 residents, it has a very high proportion of parliamentary representation, it forgets that the elected representatives cannot initiate change without the consent and co-operation of the Tenants. This may, so far, not have led to any suppression of democracy, but it could do so. What is also overlooked is the fact that most Deputies have some sort of landlord/tenant relationship with a Tenant. This has to be, because the Tenants own all of the land and the Deputies must by definition live somewhere on a Tenant's land.

The forty Tenants actually "bought" their parliamentary seats when they purchased their own land. Often a substantial number do not bother to attend Chief Pleas, which, as it only meets routinely three times a year, is hardly an onerous task. Thus the work of administering Sark falls on the shoulders of the few Tenants who do turn up, and to a very large degree on the elected Deputies who are in a permanent minority. Whilst minor matters are settled on a show of hands, important matters, or items likely to be the subject of contention, are settled by calling the roll.

The voting procedure in calling the roll in Chief Pleas is unusual. Each person attending is called by name, and has to state, "pour" or "contre". The first to vote is the Seigneur, the "head" of the island. Whether he intends it or not, his vote surely sets the tone because subconsciously it states, "this is my island and this is my view." The next vote is that of the Seneschal, the Seigneur's own appointee. No prizes for guessing which way he might vote. The next few to vote may be tempted to swing in behind the Seigneur and the Seneschal either on the grounds of tactical expediency or because they believe that there are plenty more votes to follow them, so why should they stick their necks out? As more and more Tenants vote in the same way, the die becomes cast so that by the time the Deputies, the only truly democratically-elected members of Chief Pleas come to vote, they may be staring a fait accompli in the face. Such a system of voting has been called intimidatory.

It can never be certain that this scenario occurs, but experience has shown the author that in similar situations voters tend to take their directions from others, either knowingly or unknowingly. Previous accounts about the domestic affairs of Sark are full of revolutionary views aired by "dissidents" outside Chief Pleas, only to see them evaporate at the vote inside Chief Pleas. There can be no doubt, that in Dame Sibyl's time, a determined and forceful "first vote" by her set the voting pattern of the meeting. There appears to be no procedure for a secret ballot at the meetings of Chief Pleas. The relegation of Deputies of the People to the last in the queue to vote does not seem logical or equitable and almost makes them "toothless tigers".

Decisions made by Chief Pleas are implemented by the Douzaine which as its name implies consists of twelve persons and has been likened to a Parish Council. The members of the Douzaine are elected by the members of Chief Pleas, from members of Chief Pleas. This incestuous arrangement prevents the possibility of any dissenters airing their views. The Douzaine are sworn under oath to secrecy, so what they talk about is never known. In turn, further duties are carried out by a series of committees.

This is where the real control of Sark lies. At the last count there appeared to be 21 committees manned by varying permutations of the same 30 persons. Tenants have a numerical superiority on 13 of the committees which by a happy chance appear to be the most important ones. A further committee is evenly split but with the Chairman (and casting vote) being a Tenant. Deputies of the People seem to be left in charge of such key committees as The Island Hall, Tree Planting and Road Traffic - in an island with no cars!

Possibly to ensure that all the committees toe the party line, there is at least one member of the Douzaine on each of the committees, apart from Tree Planting (boring?) and Housing (what housing?).

Even more startling is the fact that the Douzaine is charged with supervising the election of the Deputies of the People even to the extent of counting the votes. Granted, this latter task is carried out under the watchful eyes of the two constables, but consider the overall position in the context of the UK.

The Prime Minister and his colleagues draw up legislation. The Prime Minister and some of those same colleagues put the legislation into effect. When the time comes for elections to the Government, the Prime Minister and his colleagues count the votes. Fair play is guaranteed by two persons who are appointees approved of by the Prime Minister. Hmm!

It could be argued that Sark has not got itself into the sort of mess councils on mainland Britain have, where all the seats are elective and indeed, this would be a fair comment. However, Sark does not have to face many of the problems faced by such councils. This is not because its system of government is better, but simply because Sark is comparatively isolated even by present day standards. The island has neither public transport to consider, nor street lights, nor the provision of leisure centres, swimming pools or parks. The happy absence of cars, which has nothing to do with feudalism or seigneuralism means that a large amount of crime and expense which originate from the wretched motor vehicle simply does not happen.

Whether the present system could rise to the challenge of a real crisis remains to be seen. It is hard to see how the large amount of power vested in the hands of the Seigneur can be healthy, especially when that person is answerable to no one and indeed, the identity of the Seigneur can change in a very short time as the past history of Sark has shown. If a British-born boy-wonder, pop/football/computer star, for example, offered the Seigneur, present or future, a mind-blowing sum of money for the Fief, who is to say that he would not be tempted to sell his inheritance? The fact that such a newcomer would undoubtedly be rich does not automatically qualify him as suitable to be the Seigneur. Readers might care to speculate what the late Robert Maxwell might have made of Sark had he purchased it!

In this day and age, there is a lot of money "sloshing around" and millionaires arise from the most unlikely sources. Perhaps it is time for Sark to take stock of its possible vulnerability in this direction. Sark is much too valuable to be left to the mercy of economic whims. The economic structure of Sark is decidedly fragile. At the top is the ruling oligarchy and its clique. They make sufficient money from the Sark Lark and perhaps other undiscovered schemes to be financially insulated from the real world. Next come the hoteliers and small business owners. Whilst some may dabble in the Sark Lark, they depend heavily upon tourists. Finally there is the "underclass" who clean the rooms, tend the horses, empty the rubbish, catch the fish and mend the roads.

Tourism is clearly in decline in the Channel Islands as it is to a degree in the resorts on the mainland. People are able to get more miles for their money and thus forsake Guernsey for Greece, and bypass Sark for the Seychelles. This decline is probably unstoppable because in the case of the Channel Islands, the sheer cost of getting there puts people off.

Housing on Sark is also unbalanced. There is a dearth of affordable accommodation for the "underclass" because the value of a Sark property is not simply the economic value of the site and its accommodations, but more related to what can be done once Sark residency is established by the buyer. Currently advertised is a property which the vendor admits needs a considerable amount spending on it to make it habitable, some say £30,000, and yet in Devon one would write it off at first glance as a barn or old cowshed. The price for the Sark property is £100,000 for a 25 year repairing lease. This level of price is completely beyond the pocket of the ordinary Sarkese.

Thus Sark is a location where any reduction in visitors will affect the majority who have little say in how Sark is run, but will not affect the minority ruling classes who have other financial fish to fry.

Indeed, on Sark it is rumoured that certain senior members of the ruling junta are not particularly happy with the day trippers although willing to tolerate the longer-stay visitors.

Sark sells itself through the peace and solitude angle. This market is diminishing also. To persons of the author's age, who can recall true peace and quiet, Sark is the "bees' knees". To younger persons who have never experienced solitude and have grown up surrounded by a cacophony of sound, Sark could well be regarded as "boring". This should not be taken as a signal to Sark to join the jet set, merely a caution that nothing lasts for ever.

NEW SARK

ADVERTS ON THE INTERNET

"This package includes a company that has bearer shares and nominee directors with domicile in Sark but administration in Latvia."

"Sark is probably the only true remaining fiscal paradise in the world. Communications are excellent with some of the most sophisticated telephone and postal systems in the world."

CBS BROADCAST FROM SARK

"But a few years ago, with the dawning of the age of the "super pirate", the Sarkese discovered that the computer is mightier than the musket."

MEMBER OF CHIEF PLEAS

"A business person would not be doing very well if he could not earn a minimum of £40,000 through directorships. But I doubt if anyone involved in the off-shore service industry on Sark is earning more than £100,000. We have to make our own way without any help from the UK, so what right does England have to tell us that what we are doing is morally wrong?"

CHAPTER THIRTY-EIGHT

IN SICKNESS AND IN HEALTH

Even today, Sark has only the services of a GP to look after the island. Anything beyond the resources of the local doctor must result in the patient being transferred to Guernsey, normally by the marine ambulance, *Flying Christine*. A consultation costs £13 and a prescription £2.70, the latter being subsidised by a fund established by a philanthropic former resident, Professor Saint.

To get the patient to the harbourside will generally require the services of the "trambulance", an ingenious device where the front end is a tractor, and the rear end is a traditional ambulance. Once this has been started up, the cash register also springs into action. It costs £25 to get carted to the harbour by the ambulance. Once aboard the *Flying Christine* a further charge arises, said to be £100. Upon arrival at the hospital in Guernsey another clock starts ticking, at around £400 per bed night before any medication.

It has been represented to the author that a confinement due to pregnancy involves a cost of around £2,000, more if there are complications. It is obvious that private insurance is required to pay for medical attention and Sark has a block policy to which most, but not all, subscribe. Like similar polices in the UK, the premiums rise with the age of the policyholder and one case is known of an older couple paying £130 per month.

Pregnancy is not covered, being in the insurance world a self-inflicted "illness". Younger Sarkese seem to remain uninsured in the hope that they will keep well and their only requirement will be for pregnancy for which, of course, they have to foot the bill anyway.

At first, such a system might point the way forward for the overburdened National Health Service in the UK but upon reflection, these charges apply whether you have a job or not. For the Sark "underclass", that is, the hewers of wood and the drawers of water, the cost of insurance, coupled with the penal level of rents means most of them find life a perpetual struggle. For the Sark "upper class", i.e. the Tenants, the practitioners of the Sark Lark and the ruling oligarchy, these charges are but nothing. The English "squires" can of course decamp back to the shires and join the NHS queues. Thus they have no incentive to consider if things can be done differently.

It is beyond comprehension that rather than increase taxes by a relatively minute fraction, the Seigneur and his Sark Parliament are prepared to do nothing. It is also beyond comprehension that there exists, in the British Isles, an "underclass" which does not have free medical treatment as of right.

There is another oddity on Sark. It seems that infertile couples wishing to have children cannot adopt, at least not without great difficulty and influence. The reason is that most sources of unwanted children have a requirement for a Social Services Home Study Report before placing a child. Quite right too. However, there are no social services on Sark and Sark is reported as being completely against any social worker coming to the island in an official capacity. One wonders why.

On the subject of children a further interesting point arises. Because of the non-allowance of a local divorce, there are, it seems, quite a number of couples who live together without the blessing of the Church. As often happens, babies arrive and these are obviously illegitimate. As such, these children could not inherit.

Very recently, Sark has changed its inheritance laws. Some say this is the result of pressure from the Barclays, others, including the

Seigneur, seem to imply that this change was long over due and all that the Barclays did was to hasten it. As to which explanation is the correct one, "you pays your money and takes your choice".

However, Sark may well have adopted a poisoned chalice for itself. Whereas the eldest son inherited the Tenement by law, now a father may choose one, but only one, child to inherit. These may now include daughters and illegitimate children, which is a small but overdue advance. Thus a father with serveral children now has to make a specific choice. If he holds all of his children in equal regard, his choice will not only be difficult, but is bound to upset the children not chosen to inherit. Thus he may decide not to make a will regarding his Tenement, in which case the old law of primogeniture applies. But declining to make a choice is in fact the same as making a choice under these circumstances. Sark may well live to regret the half-way house which it has constructed.

This is truly amazing. On Sark, the Barclays are referred to in the same context as Satan. Young children are told to be good, "otherwise the Barclays will get you". Undoubtedly, somewhere on the island pins are pushed into effegies of the brothers. Yet it has taken the intervention of these two outsiders to give the Sarkese rights which should have been given decades ago. Surely someone on Sark must ask the question as to why it takes outside pressures to obtain rights which everybody else in the British Isles enjoys and, more to the point, what other rights are out there yet to be won? Perhaps the right to be protected against unfair dismissal, or eviction, or harassment?

It is possible, on Sark, for a person to lose long standing employment for daring to raise his voice in criticism. There is no redress. It is also possible for that same person to then find himself homeless, if, through the complex and incestuous network of committees which run Sark, pressure is able to be brought on his landlord. Again, there is no redress.

If the victim cannot find alternative work or accommodation, and as a "marked" man, this would be difficult, (as was found by

William Toplis) his alternative would be either to live in the open air and starve, or go to the UK and throw himself on the mercy of the state. This would amount to a de facto "deportation" from one of the Queen's territories. This scenario has happened. It is not fiction.

Some years ago, a Deputy suggested that if Sark were to build just one house a year for "social housing" in twenty years it would have, at relatively low cost, a pool of housing to meet the needs of those who have fallen on hard times. She was told, "there is no need, Sark looks after its own." Sark's motto must surely be, "the rich man in his castle, the poor man at the gate" Marie Antoinette would have found much in Sark to reassure her that all had not been lost in the French Revolution.

In recent years, there has been another player in the emergency assistance field. The Barclays of Brecqhou have a helicopter which they freely make available, to any of the Channel Islands which have need of it. Whether it be gorse fires in Jersey or Sark, ships in distress at sea or lifting casualties to hospital when the *Flying Christine* cannot put to sea, the Brecqhou helicopter turns out.

This is as it should be. As President Roosevelt said to Congress during the famous Lend-Lease debates, *"If my neighbour's house is on fire, would I not lend him my hose?"* However, before the Brecqhou helicopter can assist Sark, permission has to be sought from the Seigneur. Should he not be available the rescue operation becomes stalled. This cannot be right. In an emergency, all "red tape" should be put on hold. The important thing is to get help to where it is needed as quickly as possible except, it seems, on feudal Sark.

Mention of fires brings to mind the Sark Fire Brigade. Until the late 1920's, there were no fire appliances on Sark. Then Guernsey presented the island with a redundant hand-operated fire pump. This was duly shipped over to Sark and unloaded at Creux Harbour. There it stayed and stayed and stayed.

Sark was quite unable to organise the transportation of the appliance to the top of Harbour Hill and place it in service. One day, someone removed the chocks and it gently trundled down the slope and into the sea. Jokers in

Guernsey placed on display a watering-can inscribed "Sark Fire Service".

Things are better now, although the lack of water mains does make carrying water to the fire difficult. However, since fire is no respecter of rank, and real property is dear to the hearts of the ruling clique, some money has been spent on a Fire Service.

ANYTHING FOR THE WEEKEND, SIR?

One might be forgiven for thinking that in feudal Sark, the absence of the day-to-day pressures of the twentieth century might have a beneficial effect on the more intimate side of human relationships. This appears not to be the case, for Sark seems to be the Viagra Capital of the United Kingdom. This wonder drug which, at the time of writing, is virtually unobtainable on the mainland, can be obtained quite freely via Sark.

Out at the northern end of Sark, a "one man and a dog operation" (quite literally) is busy bringing instant relief to the sufferings of UK Man. Often seen scooting to Guernsey and back in his rigid inflatable boat, sometimes in terrible weather, this man deserves our grateful thanks for showing the true benefits of feudalism,

> "It was brandy for the parson
> and baccy for the clerk
> Now it's Viagra for the nation
> God bless the Isle of Sark"

With sincere apologies to the late John Masefield.

CHAPTER THIRTY-NINE

LET THERE BE LIGHT

For better or worse, the second World War undoubtedly changed the attitude of the man in the street both as to political power and to what could be achieved when everyone pulls together for a common cause. New attitudes coupled with new technology threw light into dark corners and raised expectations of better things now that hostilities had ended. Except of course, on Sark.

In 1947, a Mr J Robson came to Sark from Wolverhampton to start the "Robson Electric Supply Co." on an island where, apart from about eighteen privately-owned generators, there was no supply of electricity. By 1953, the number of private generators had dropped to three and the Company had 150 customers. The Power Station, to give it a rather grand title, was, and still is, situated almost at the top of Harbour Hill close to the Hotel Aval du Creux and in 1953 housed six diesel generators producing some 60KW at 220 volts DC.

Of course, Sark being Sark, Robson often had complaints about the proximity of his power lines causing apple trees to fail to fruit and a lady who complained that the milk kept cold in an electric fridge gave her family colic. Another man sympathised at the loss of power occasioned by windy days when, in his view, the wind blew the electricity off the power line!

Unfortunately these amusing asides were but nothing to the abuse and harassment to which Robson was subjected, by those who controlled Sark. Robson had entered the political mainstream of Sark, first being elected as a Deputy of the People and then, by virtue of his purchase of the Tenement of Aval du Creux, gaining his automatic seat in Chief Pleas.

Of course, Sark could not let Robson get on with the job. A committee had to be formed to be known as "The Electricity Committee" comprising La Dame, the Seneschal (a retired bank manager) and Mr Head. Their knowledge of electricity was probably restricted to "Homes Law" i.e. plug in and switch on.

The Sarkese disliked Robson for no other reason than that he had skills none of them possessed; he had an ability to make money and he clearly saw the solutions to Sark's energy problems. And of course, he was not Sark-born!

In 1949, Robson brought to the island sixty wooden electric light poles. This resulted in one the stormiest meetings of Chief Pleas anyone could remember. For 45 minutes, a heated debate raged between Seneschal Baker and Henry Head. Tempers became frayed. There were references to a "Fifth Column within Sark", "swindles", "judicial and legislative irregularities" and a call for a formal enquiry to be conducted by the Lieutenant Governor. All over a load of wooden poles!

The debate was started by the Seneschal saying that the electric light poles should be pulled down as no approval had been given for them to be erected. It was pointed out that Mr Robson had been given formal permission to import the poles into Sark for the purpose of furthering his electrical business and that by clever deduction, it could be inferred that eventually they would be moved into a vertical position.

It was proposed by the Seneschal and seconded by Mr Charles Perrée of Little Sark, that the poles should be returned to the horizontal position. It was then pointed out that such poles as had been erected were on private property and could not be removed by order of Chief Pleas.

The question of the poles was serious enough to need a special session of Chief Pleas. Those supporting Robson pointed out that he had been given permission to import the poles which were then hauled up to the top of Harbour Hill. Subsequently, they were placed alongside holes in the hedges and it must have been clear to even the most simple-minded Sarkese, what the ultimate purpose was. It was only when the poles were erected and the wires strung along the tops that the objectors came out of hiding.

The Guernsey Evening Press summed it all up rather nicely, *"It is all very well to make Sark a showplace for tourists but when the personal comfort of many inhabitants has to be sacrificed on this account it is carrying zeal a little too far. Sark, like the rest of the world, cannot afford to lag too far behind the times. Nobody would care to see its unique constitution and way of life tampered with, but it is impossible to remain completely medieval nowadays and often distinctly uncomfortable to attempt it."*

Robson got his poles up and the business went from strength to strength. In 1962, Robson repaired and tested Dame Sibyl Hathaway's new electric wheelchair and sensibly decided to take it for a short spin to ensure it functioned correctly and safely.

Summoned to the Court of Sark, he was fined £2 with the words, *"I think it is utterly reprehensible that you should have a lapse of this kind. You are a member of this island's legislative body and a deputy of the people. You must know that it was not long ago that the island parliament met to consider the legislation which is in hand."*

The case was heard before the Deputy Seneschal (H Bell, La Dame's son-in-law) who caused amusement by referring to John Malcolm Robson, as John Malcolm Campbell when reading out the charges.

A law had been passed allowing La Dame to have an electric wheelchair but had not yet been placed on the statute book, which was quite reason enough to prosecute Robson.

One wonders what would have happened if Mr Robson had declined to test the carriage and La Dame had accidentally driven over a cliff because of an undetected defect!

In 1962, Robson, clearly a glutton for punishment, floated the idea of Sark having a Public Water Supply. The island drew its water from boreholes, most of which were polluted to some degree and Robson's idea was to have a central main drawing water from previously untapped sources to be pumped into each home by electric pumps. The idea of paying for pure water when water of questionable quality was available for free was not looked upon as a good deal by Sark, so the project foundered.

In 1963, an electrical war broke out on Sark. Having "wired up" virtually the whole of Great Sark, Robson moved his cables and poles down to Little Sark. At great personal expense, he carried the supply across La Coupée, underground so as not to spoil the beauty of this causeway, and stood ready to bring electric light to the few houses on Little Sark. On the Little Sark side of La Coupée, he brought the cable back to the surface and erected a pole on which to attach a transformer.

At once, there was a furious objection to the pole which seemed to have been put up on land owned by Phillip Perrée. The Sark Court ordered that the pole be removed. The Constable of Sark, one Tom Hincks, threatened to have Robson locked up in the Sark gaol if the pole was not removed. The pole was duly relocated onto a property named La Moiserie but Mr Perrée could still see it and vowed that he would not have any of Robson's electricity, neither would his Tenants. Hincks, the gung-ho constable, then decided he was selling his property and, realising that it would fetch a better price "on the mains" rather than off, signed up for a supply of Robson's current.

At this point, the Listers, who rented La Sablonnerie Hotel from Mr Perrée decided to share some of their "home-made" electricity with their neighbours. Mr Perrée was helpful in supplying the cable to connect up with La Sablonnerie. No price was too high to keep Robson out of Little Sark.

An empty cable drum was placed at La Coupée with the message, *"Get Out Robson"* painted across it in large white letters.

However, the offending pole still stood on La Moiserie land which Perrée could not control. Then La Moiserie came up for sale and Perrée invoked the law of "retraite" whereby persons to certain specified degrees of affinity with the vendor, can acquire the property at the agreed price. After a hearing in the Sark Court, "retraite" was awarded to Perrée who then became the owner of the land on which the pole was situated and promptly told Robson to remove the pole. Little Sark eventually succumbed to the lure of mains electricity and became the largest customers of the Sark Electricity Company.

In 1964, John Robson was concerned that the rather "hit and miss" arrangements which characterised his involvement with Sark, ought to be formalised as they were in Guernsey, that is by an Order-in-Council which safeguarded both the supplier and the customer. As things stood, Robson could just shut up shop and leave Sark in the lurch. On the other side of the coin, under Sark's antiquated property laws, future purchasers of Tenements might well require the electricity poles to be removed. What Robson wished was some form of statutory backing which protected everyone. He had made seven attempts to obtain an Order-in-Council, without any luck and so, on 30th September 1964, he deliberately cut the power for 36 minutes to let Sark experience what it would be like to revert to candles and wood fires. He soon obtained the required documentation!

On 31st December 1970, John Robson sold the enterprise and retired to concentrate on his other hobby, yachting.

PART TWO

BRECQHOU

BRECQHOU IS IN THE
HAPPY POSITION OF BEING
AN ISLAND WITHOUT A
HISTORY

CHAPTER FORTY

SETTING THE SCENE
1309-1677

If the average Briton was asked to name all of the Channel Islands, he would rapidly reel off Jersey and Guernsey, (slight pause), Sark, (slight pause), Alderney. He might just recall Herm, but thereafter, his mind would be a blank. Few would be able to name Jethou, Lihou, Burhou, Minquières Casquets and the Ile de Chausey, let alone Brecqhou.

This is not at all surprising. After all, in the summer of 1902, the English botanist, Cecil P Hurst, spent a week studying the flora of history and then pronounced it as *"being in the happy position of an island without a history."* He can be forgiven, because his field of study was botany, but he could not have been more in error when it came to Brecqhou. The problem is that the history of the island has never been recorded before apart from generally inaccurate fragments in other books about Sark.

The island of Brecqhou (variously known as Brechou, Brehoc, Brekhou, Bryhoc and Ile aux Marchants), is almost due west of Sark, separated from its larger neighbour by the Gouliot Passage, a narrow strip of water merely 80 metres across but often a veritable maelstrom to navigate.

Rumour has it that in 1939 a British destroyer was carefully inched through the Gouliot Passage pushing against the flood tide. Possible yes, but unlikely that a captain would have hazarded his ship for no good reason. Again, in the summer of 1968, an unknown destroyer is reputed to have made the same journey. Of course, to a landsman, any ship with a gun at the front is a destroyer if not a cruiser, so it may well have been a fishery protection minesweeper taking a short cut!

Some 87 acres in extent Brecqhou is almost one sixteenth the size of Sark. Looking fairly barren at first glance, it does have quite a fertile soil. Early usage tended to be restricted to grazing sheep and cattle but from time to time, the land has been farmed.

Some seventy-six species of birds have been recorded on Brecqhou, ranging from the common herring gull to the not so common bee-eater. In addition, some thirty-seven species of beetle have been located as well as three species of moth. Over two hundred and ninety flowers and plants have been listed as growing on Brecqhou, including twenty-six specimens not previously recorded on Sark. Finally there were at one time eighty-five trees growing but this number has diminished. It is almost impossible for a young tree to withstand the gales and the most sturdy trees which have flourished are sycamore and tamarisk. However, when it is recalled that in Tudor times, Sark was also without trees, there is hope for Brecqhou yet.

Brecqhou was at one time part of the Fief of Vinchelez in Jersey. This may seem odd, since Jersey is some 20 miles distant and on the other side of Sark and one would be forgiven for assuming that Sark or Guernsey might have been a more logical partner. However, until about 1290 AD, there was only one Bailiwick of the Channel Islands and thus there was no anomaly in having a part of a Jersey fief adjacent to Guernsey. The Fief of Vinchelez was purchased by Nicholas de Chesney whose son Guillaume inherited it in 1326. In due course, his son, Edmund de Chesney inherited the property and when he died, around 1340, a Contract of Partage was executed whereby all the fiefs, estates and lands belonging to Sir Edmund were divided amongst his five co-heirs, Joanne, Eleanor, Isabel, Ralph and Nicholas who were all minors. The Fief de Vinchelez, but excluding Brecqhou, went to Eleanor. Joanne ended up owning Brecqhou, and then later married a

Guernseyman named Denis le Marchant. The Fief de Vinchelez then became divided and fragmented among daughters and thereby lost its noble knight-tenure status. Technically, Brecqhou would have been required to contribute towards the 10 sol rente but proportionately this would have been small and seems to have withered on the vine. If payable it would have been due to Jersey, with all the consequent difficulties of collection and enforcement.

The le Marchant family had a penchant for putting their names to everything they owned, and Brecqhou became in time known as Ile aux Marchants.

Title to Brecqhou passed by inheritance down the Le Marchant family line until, in 1677, we find ownership of Brecqhou passing to Dame Rachel le Moigne as executrix for her minor son, William. The important point to note is that in 1677, Brecqhou indisputably belonged to the Le Marchant family who were Tenants-in-Chief of the Crown, i.e. freeholders, to use English parlance, and the island was not part of the Fief or Manor of Sark.

This distinction is critical. Brecqhou is geologically part of Sark. Brecqhou comes under the same ecclesiastical jurisdiction as Sark. The pivotal point is that Brecqhou is not part of the Fief or Manor of Sark - an administrative difference which has wide repercussions.

This then sets the background for the first battle for Brecqhou which will be explored in depth in the next chapter.

CHAPTER FORTY-ONE

PHILIPPE DE CARTERET POUNCES
1675-1681

In October 1675 Philippe de Carteret, newly arrived on Sark and like most young men raring to make his mark on life decided to tour his new fiefdom. Pausing for a while on the west coast, he saw sheep grazing on the adjacent island of Brecqhou. When being informed that they belonged to the Le Marchant family, he ordered them to be removed by his agent.

Thus ended a good month for young Philippe. He had dealt with the Bishop of Winchester to regularise the parish status and incumbency of Sark and had also commenced litigation in the Royal Court against those Tenants who had sub-divided their Tenements in complete disregard of the Letters Patent of 1611.

Indeed, since coming into his inheritance, he had been a really active "new broom". The death of Elie Brévint in 1674 probably removed a brake on change in Sark because in 1675 de Carteret obtained Letters Patent for a new structure for the Sark Court. In the following year he was instrumental in getting the defences of Sark inspected by an army officer. In October 1677, he obtained an ordinance from the Royal Court prohibiting the taking of eggs and birds from the rocks around Sark.

When word of the removal of her sheep got back to Dame Rachel Le Moigne (Madame le Marchant) she was not at all pleased. As the widow of James Le Marchant and guardian/tutrice of his children, she had a legal duty to protect their assets. Thus she brought an action in the Royal Court of Guernsey on 4th December 1677 claiming to be the owner of Brecqhou.

It seems clear that at the outset, young de Carteret thought that Brecqhou belonged to him by right, that is to say, it was part and parcel of the Fief of Sark granted to Helier de Carteret by the Charter of 1565 because in December, the Court ordered that *"the Seigneur's Patent was to be examined"*.

Regrettably from Dame Rachel's viewpoint, it was also known that some of the older title deeds to Brecqhou had been lost by the Le Marchants. A Royal Commission had pinpointed this fact in 1597. Thus there existed a situation between de Carteret who *thought* that Brecqhou belonged to him but was unable to substantiate his claim and Dame Rachel, who knew Brecqhou belonged to her family, but had lost some of the title deeds.

As the case moved on, de Carteret dropped any reference to the 1565 Charter in his pleading over Brecqhou but presented the same Charter in support of his litigation with Tenants, which helpfully appears to have been heard with the Brecqhou case. The inference which can be drawn from this omission is that de Carteret had by now realised that the 1565 Charter was of no use to him in his Brecqhou pleadings.

This is very significant. One does not decline to use a Royal Charter, then one of the most powerful documents available, unless one believes it to be unhelpful and not relevant to one's case. Indeed, a Royal Charter, sealed with the Great Seal of England would have been a "gilt-edged, copper-bottomed, A1 at Lloyd's" piece of evidence yet de Carteret only used it in support of his other litigation, to which of course it was very relevant.

However, as will be seen in the first part of this book, Helier de Carteret had originally farmed Sark on a "fee ferme" basis, a short renewable lease. This was logical, for until de Carteret could satisfy himself that Sark was an economic proposition, there was no point in entering into more permanent arrangements. When, in his petition to Queen Elizabeth I, he sought that Sark be placed on the same basis as St Ouen, he specifically referred to the land he already farmed as fee ferme. This did not include Brecqhou.

At the same time, Dame Rachel was given three months' grace by the Court to take instructions from William, who seems to have come of age during the currency of the case and was away in England. This consideration shown by the Court points to an eventual agreed settlement rather than an enforced judgement.

There was further proof that Brecqhou was not part of the Fief of Sark. When the case of Le Marchant v de Carteret got underway, de Carteret sought permission for the action to be joined by the Crown but was adjudged "à silence". This is the legal expression indicating that the Crown could not join in the case because it had no legal interest in the outcome.

Had Brecqhou been part of Sark, then the Crown would have had the same legal interest in Brecqhou as it undoubtedly had in Sark and would have been admitted as a joint defendant with de Carteret. The Crown clearly knew that Brecqhou was owned by the Le Marchant family that it was not part of the territory intended to be transferred to de Carteret in 1565, and to put it bluntly, it was no business of the Crown to get involved. At the time, the Lord Chief Justice of England was Lord Coke who gave the world the famous expression, "An Englishman's home is his castle". It would hardly be likely that an administration which held such noble views, would expropriate an adjoining island merely to satisfy a minor squire from the Channel Islands.

After the expiry of the three months, both parties were ordered to appear before the Court and *"to bring their proofs and aids, if they have any"*. There followed a settlement, blessed by the Court, whereby Dame Rachel relinquished her rights in Brecqhou to de Carteret.

The phrase, *"relinquished her rights"* is written into the records of the Royal Court and it is a most revealing piece of evidence. One can only relinquish one's rights if one has them in the first place. Had the Le Marchants been mere "squatters", the Court would have ordered them off without further ado. It is not known exactly why Dame Rachel did this, although an educated guess is that she was a relatively impoverished woman, and the monies she paid to the Crown for the defence of Brecqhou were not covered by the income from grazing sheep on the island.

In short, Brecqhou, with its attendant defence obligations, was more of a liability to her than an asset. Certainly, the present head of the Le Marchant family says that it is a family tradition that they lost Brecqhou because they could not afford the cost of defending it. There is irrefutable evidence that the Crown did receive separate revenues from Brecqhou between 1642 and 1649 and this fact alone is very significant. If Brecqhou had been part of the Fief of Sark during those years, it could not have yielded any revenues to the Crown. The revenue devolving to the Crown from Sark was of course the 50 shillings per year mentioned in the 1565 Charter and if Brecqhou was encompassed within Sark, no other source of Crown revenue could have originated from Brecqhou.

There is in existence a very important account of State (formerly Crown) revenues dated 1649 which lists all income due, including rents from Brecqhou. At the end of the list, it shows separately, revenue from Sark, formerly Sir Philippe de Carteret's, now forfeit to the State. This very clearly separates Brecqhou from Sark for the latter island was forfeit by virtue of the de Carterets' loyalty to the Crown.

Brecqhou was very much a "happy hunting-ground" for Sarkese in search of rabbits. In 1673, there was published in London a tract entitled, "News from The Channel". The author was a Londoner, one F Wearis who seems to have spent some time on Sark before and during the Civil War period. Wearis was a keen observer of what would now be called the "nitty gritty" and he makes the following comments:

"*Of Conies (rabbits) we have everywhere exceeding plenty, and yet, lest we should want, Nature has provided us with a particular Warren placing at a small distance in the sea, an island of about half a mile every way over, which is inhabited by nothing else whither we commonly go a Ferreting and have them in such abundance that is has been confidently told me that some Families here have made £15 or £20 a year only of their Skins*"

This obviously irritated the Le Marchant family because on at least two occasions the matter was brought before the Royal Court of Guernsey with judgements going against Sark.

For example, on 19th May 1638, the Court ordered, "*at the instance of Henry Bird, Tenant of the Isle of Brecqhou and on the complaint he had made of the abuse he has suffered by the inhabitants of the Isle of Sercq, whereby all persons are prohibited from going to the Isle of Brecqhou to hunt or to take rabbits on penalty of 18 sous recompense to his Majesty, or to the profit of the said Tenant, in accordance with previous ordonnances in this case.*"

This report of a law case is sufficient alone to prove that Brecqhou was not part of Sark. If Mr Henry Bird described as a Tenant was in fact a Tenant in the Sark sense of the word, he would have had a seat in Chief Pleas. In fact in 1638, there was no member of Chief Pleas of that name. Furthermore, consider the language used. It is a complaint by the inhabitant of one island against the depredations of inhabitants of another quite separate island, almost like two foreign countries in fact. Had Brecqhou been part of Sark, the language used would have been different. Finally, there is a reference to any fines levied going to the King. All that the King received from Sark was fifty shillings a year. However in 1638, Brecqhou was temporarily back in the hands of the Crown which was letting it out to make good deficiencies on the defence account rendered to the Le Marchants but unpaid.

Additionally on Saturday 29th July 1665, *By Messrs James de Havilland, Jean de Samarès, Daniel de Beauvoir and Elizar de Samarès, all Jurats, James Le Marchant was granted permission to have published in Guernsey and in the Isle of Sark, a notice that no persons may go to the ferret or to shoot his rabbits on his Isle des Marchants upon penalty of £10.*

This is conclusive evidence that long after the Charter of 1565, the island of Brecqhou was totally outside the jurisdiction of the Sark Court. The final phrase in the second judgement is most significant, "on his Isle des Marchants" Indeed, had Brecqhou been part of Sark, the plaintiff would have been the Seigneur of Sark or perhaps another member or Quarantaine and the Sark Court would have been the recipient of the fines levied.

In the 16th century, there were many alarms and excursions in the Channel Islands about the possibility of attack from the French and the Crown sought contributions, directly or indirectly, from the owners/inhabitants for the defence budget. It is also clearly documented that where owners failed to take adequate preparations against invasion, the Crown was entitled to carry out the work and retain the revenue from those lands to recoup the cost. Lundy Island in the Bristol Channel is a case in point where this was actually done, and Alderney carries a well-documented threat to do the same.

Exactly when the Crown stepped in to recover defence costs from Brecqhou is not precisely known, but during the period 1629-1649, the Crown Receiver on Guernsey recorded revenue from Brecqhou. The inference is that a lease, probably of 21 years was granted in order to generate income from which the Crown could recoup its outlay.

The income produced was £2 per year plus two barrels of samphire for the Brecqhou grazing rights. Samphire was a product of the Brecqhou cliffs and was exported to Rouen where it was used as a flavouring and a herb for pickling. The two barrels diverted to the Receiver in Guernsey were probably a perquisite of the Office.

This would neatly align with the fact that the first court judgement referred to above and dated 1638, refers to a Tenant, Henry Bird. The second judgement, dated 1665, and outside the period of the lease, refers to James le Marchant. Clearly by 1665, all defence dues had been paid, and le Marchant regained the economic use of his island.

Samphire was so highly prized that Sarkese were often on Brecqhou stealing this plant. In 1616, the Royal Court of Guernsey confirmed the arrest of Abraham Vaudin of Sark. In this case, the rights to the samphire were held by Pierre Pipet and exercised via Pierre de la Rue, a "fermier" of Brecqhou. Again, in 1625, Timotée Vaudin, a resident of Guernsey, took Thomas de Carteret and Thomas Poingdextre to court claiming that bracken and samphire had been wrongly taken by them from Brecqhou.

On 1st April 1799, the Royal Court in Guernsey heard an application from *"Pierre Le Pelley, Ecuyer, Seigneur de l'isle de Serk et* **propriétaire de l'isle de Brecqhou"** regarding the age-old problem of illegal rabbiting. The bold portion shows that Le Pelley fully realised the fine distinction of being the Seigneur of Sark but only the owner of Brecqhou. Similar wording was used again in 1807, and both of these decisions of the Royal Court were transmitted to and registered in the Sark Greffe.

Even closer to the present day, when legislation was passed in 1935 for the registration of births and deaths it was expressly stipulated that for the *purposes of that legislation,* Brecqhou was to be considered part of Sark, clear evidence that in the minds of legislators Brecqhou was not part of Sark. Were it otherwise, there would have been no need to have made this stipulation.

A casual reading of these events might well lead to the perfectly reasonable conclusion that whilst Brecqhou could not have been part of the Fief of Sark in 1565, perhaps it was from 1681 onwards. Not so. Brecqhou was not subsequently sub-infeudated into the Fief of Sark. If it had been, it would have involved positive action by the Crown. A further Royal Charter would have been required. No such action has been recorded or even hinted at in any documents.

The fact that a person who as Lord of one Manor subsequently acquires a piece of adjacent land does not automatically place the new acquisition into that Manor. Only the Crown can do that. In any case, there would be no motive in de Carteret giving back to the Crown a piece of land to which he had recently acquired absolute title. The procedure of sub-infeudation would not have escaped de Carteret's notice because in 1640, another Jersey Fief was incorporated into his own Fief of St Ouen by Letters Patent, so he well knew the drill.

The only sustainable conclusion has to be that from 1681, Philippe de Carteret acquired the rights of Dame Rachel Le Marchant, as *"Tenant-in-Chief of the Crown"* in respect of the island of Brecqhou, in addition to, **but separate from**, his Seigneuries of St Ouen and Sark. From this, there then follows the inescapable conclusion that whatever peculiar rules governed Sark, with regard to inheritance for example, these could not apply to Brecqhou. Owning a piece of real estate by way of being Tenant-in-Chief of the Crown is as near to being freehold as makes no difference. This had more important implications for later battles over this tiny island.

A further point is why it took from 1565 until 1681 before the de Carterets made a move upon Brecqhou. Logically, if Helier de Carteret had thought Brecqhou was part of a newly granted Fief in 1565, he would have granted the island as a Tenement or perhaps as a couple of Tenements from the outset. The authors of books about Sark who have listed the original forty Tenants, omit any mention of Brecqhou or of a Tenant assigned to that island.

The truth appears to be that Philippe de Carteret was an opportunist and he took a gamble which came off in his favour. Indeed there is some evidence, in his own hand, that he knew that Brecqhou was not part of Sark. In 1677, the very year that he commenced his campaign against Dame Rachel he wrote to the Bishop of Winchester.

This letter is dated 22nd October 1677 and concerns the appointment of a new priest. In it, Sir Philippe de Carteret says *"Queen Elisabeth gave my Ancestors a little island desert called Serck on condition that he should people it with such quantity of familys etc."*

Not, it should be noted, "two islands", or "these islands".

Throughout the letter he continues to use the expression

"island" in the singular. This letter, taken with the terms and expressions used in the Charter of 1565 represents further proof that all that was granted to Helier de Carteret was the island of Sark excluding Brecqhou.

Supporters of the opposite view might well say that Brecqhou was so small that it was taken for granted that it was bundled in with Sark. Not so. At Burghley House (the home of Lord Cecil) there exists to this day an atlas said to be Queen Elizabeth's personal property on which she recorded all the Crown's land grants. Sark and Brecqhou are shown separately.

Good Queen Bess well knew what she was doing in 1565 and giving away Brecqhou was not part of it.

CHAPTER FORTY-TWO

UNDER NEW MANAGEMENT
1681-1929

Once the de Carteret family had acquired Brecqhou from
Dame Rachel le Marchant, they did not do very much with it. Indeed,
very little is known about what went on after 1681. Since it was devoid
of habitation, it was most probably simply used for grazing cattle.

What is not generally known is that when in 1713 Sir Charles
de Carteret obtained Crown Licence to bequeath Sark to Trustees,
Brecqhou was never mentioned. Thus Brecqhou continued to be in the
ownership of the de Carteret family (although they probably never
realised it!) beyond the date on which Sark came under the control of
Le Pelleys. Indeed, title to Brecqhou was only established by the Le
Pelley family around 1770 by their having obtained 40 years'
unchallenged possession of the island, i.e. obtained a title by
prescription (squatter's rights).

An old guide book to the Channel Islands makes the following
observations. "A few sheep are kept on Brecqhou. In 1836, Mr Peter le
Pelley, Seigneur of Sark, broke up about 50 vergees of land, built a
house known as the "farm house" and established two families, the
Amys and the de Carterets for society and companionship. But it is a
singular fact that two families have never been able to live there in
peace for any length of time." In fact, the island was let out in 1844 at
a rent of £40 per annum.

In the latter half of the 19th century, Brecqhou was recommended as an ideal place to go for picnics which brought some much needed company for the few inhabitants. Picnickers would hire a boat at Havre Gosselin and land on the south east corner of the island. Climbing up the relatively easy grade they came across the one house and farm from which bacon and eggs were obtained. Hopefully, the Sark boatmen would return at six o'clock to take them back to Sark. Given the vagaries of the weather and the tidal rips of the Gouliot Passage, this would have been quite an ambitious outing for Victorian ladies to undertake.

Regardless of the strictures about more than one family being in occupation of Brecqhou, in 1857 Kelly's Post Office Directory reported that there were still two families settled on Brecqhou so perhaps life was not as bad after all. In 1876 a family from Guernsey, called Naftel moved onto the island and lived there until 1881. For the next twenty years, the island was used for cattle grazing by the Best family, well-known butchers of Guernsey.

In 1901 a married couple with four children were put on Brecqhou as caretakers for a Mr Badiar. They lasted for five years but from 1906 to 1911, no-one lived there at all. In November 1911 George Sharp from Alderney was granted a lease (some say for 60 years although it is thought for 50 years only) by Seigneur Collings (Dame Sibyl's father) and he arrived well loaded with furniture, dairy and farming implements, a fine assortment of farm animals and a few cats. In addition there were three members of his family, together with a carpenter. Livestock were transferred onto the island by the simple expedient of letting them swim ashore.

Amongst the animals imported into Brecqhou were some Belgian hares and, as is their wont, they bred copiously with the indigenous rabbit, producing a healthy strain of "habbits (?)" said to be better pelted and certainly more flavoursome than their cousins on Sark or Guernsey.

George Sharp had only one eye and as a result became known

as the Cyclops of Brecqhou. He was married to Agnes Lanyon the Sark schoolteacher and aunt of Hubert Lanyon, hero of the Guernsey Underground Press. Because Sharp was born in the UK, he was deported by the Germans but returned to Sark after the war. He died in 1962.

A slight digression is needed to discuss a notable personage who dearly wished to buy Brecqhou but was denied the chance. William A Toplis was a successful Sark artist with many paintings accepted by the Royal Academy. He did some research on the status of Brecqhou and concluded, correctly, that it was not part of the Fief of Sark. His plan was to buy Brecqhou from the Seigneur and declare Independence. In the meantime, he started secretly drawing plans of the island for living quarters to be erected thereon. He realised that there was silver on the island and he planned to extract it. Rumours of his prospecting activities reached the ears of Seigneur Collings who demanded that Toplis disclose the whereabouts of his discovery, because, as Seigneur Collings said, "all minerals belong to me". Toplis emphatically refused and told Collings that if in fact, all minerals did belong to the Seigneur, then he ought to know where all his minerals were kept!

Seigneur Collings refused to sell Brecqhou on the grounds that it was leased to George Sharp. When Collings's daughter did sell Brecqhou, Toplis described it as, *"an attempt to legitimise Sark's annexation of Brecqhou"* which as it turns out was a very prescient statement.

In 1929 George Sharp found to his surprise that Brecqhou was being sold from under him. In a rather pained letter to the Guernsey Evening Press in March of that year he pointed out that he, and not anyone else, would hold any seat in Chief Pleas as he held the land. There was definitely underhand work practised by Dame Sibyl here. Sharp was not willing to leave; indeed, he sent his family over to Brecqhou to harvest up the potato crop so that the incomer would not reap what Sharp had sowed. The best guess is that Sharp's lease in 1910 was sealed, as was customary in those days, by nothing more than a handshake between him and Seigneur Collings. It is known that Dame Sibyl tried to break the lease because she took legal advice from Ambrose (later Sir Ambrose) Sherwell to find a way of getting Sharp off Brecqhou. Her view was that as the lease was not registered in the Sark Greffe Office it did not exist. Thus, as someone who was not a direct party to the lease, she could repudiate it. Mr Sherwell soon showed her the error of her ways. His opinion was that an unregistered lease was protected from the landlord and the heirs of the landlord, notwithstanding the fact it was not formally registered.

It is thought that Sharp must have later relinquished the remainder of his lease to Angelo Clarke, a hotelier from Staines in Middlesex, whose stated aim was to promote his hobby as a dog breeder. How Clarke intended to get round the rule that only the Seigneur could keep unspeyed bitches is not known. Clarke approached Sibyl Beaumont who was then La Dame, with a view to acquiring the freehold. This was duly sold to Clarke for the sum of £1,400.

Thus, in 1929, Angelo Clarke, held both the **Freehold** and the **Leasehold** interests in Brecqhou, a situation which is crystal clear yet which led to considerable legal activity in the 1980's and 1990's. Dame Sibyl Beaumont, as she then was, did a curious thing.

Although Dame Sibyl held Brecqhou as Tenant-in-Chief of the Crown and was thus free to sell it without asking permission from anyone, for some reason she chose to ignore this fact. When contemplating a possible sale she wrote to the Law Officers in Guernsey stating that Crown consent was not necessary to sell Brecqhou and properties on Little Sark because they *"did not form part of the original Manor of Sark"*.

She was absolutely correct in the case of Brecqhou but totally wrong in the case of Little Sark. It is however very clear why she thought that Little Sark was also hers to sell at will. The Seigneurie records show that Little Sark was purchased in 1676. Thus the common link between Brecqhou and Little Sark is that they were, in

215

her eyes, both acquired **after** 1565.

What she did not know was that in 1645, Philippe de Carteret's grandfather had sold Little Sark complete with all Seigneurial rights, to his cousin, Sir George Carteret. This contract was passed in the Jersey Court on 26th June 1645 and included the words, "tous autres droits de seigneurie". In 1676, Philippe de Carteret repurchased Little Sark by means of a Deed of Bargain & Sale, in the English language and form, sealed in the Lord Mayor and Alderman's Court in the Guildhall London on 27th May 1676.

It will therefore be seen that the 1676 acquisition was not a fresh purchase, but a "reversing" transaction which, in theory, restored the status quo as regards Little Sark.

Whether in fact the status quo was thus restored is open to doubt. One interpretation of feudal law is that it was not. Interestingly, whilst Little Sark was "away", the Sark Court was erected in its modern form and it is debatable whether the writ of the Sark Court, even now, actually runs on Little Sark.

No matter. The position in 1929 was, as it always has been, that Brecqhou was a virtual freehold and yet Dame Sibyl pretended it was not. She then invested Brecqhou with a seat in Chief Pleas, the island's parliament and overnight, Angelo Clarke became an un-elected Member of Parliament. Where had his seat come from?

On 10th February 1835, the then Seigneur bought-in the Tenement of La Moinerie de Haut. The house was demolished shortly afterwards and the land incorporated into the demesne lands. Taken together, these events would seem to indicate that at that date, the Tenement, together with the seat in Chief Pleas appurtenant to that Tenement, had ceased to exist. This would certainly have been the case under English Manorial law. In any event, the demolition of the house and the incorporation of the land into the demesne land would indicate a very clear intent on the part of the then Seigneur that the Tenement should cease to exist in 1835.

The right to sit in Chief Pleas, restricted to the original 40

216

Tenements and their successors in title, was originally granted by custom. However, the Sark Reform Law of 1922 as re-enacted by the 1951 law gave legal status to the Tenements as they existed in 1922. The 1922 law did not however specify either the Tenements or the Tenants. On the other hand, there is no machinery contained within the 1922 law for either the extinguishment of Tenements or the transfer of seats in Chief Pleas. It speaks volumes for the calibre of Chief Pleas that no-one seems to have challenged La Dame as to what right she had to present them with a new colleague, especially one who took his seat 364 years late!

The conclusion must be that what La Dame did in 1929 was ultra vires and that there was no legal basis for investing Angelo Clarke as a Member of Chief Pleas. So why then did she do it? It is not known. Possibly she was advised by her lawyers that creating a bogus Tenement would avoid the need to obtain Crown permission. It is certainly unlikely that they would have known as much about Brecqhou as is known today.

Possibly she thought that by creating Brecqhou as a fictitious Tenement she might be preserving a future stream of Treizième. This has certainly proved to be the case, although each Treizième received by her and her grandson has been, to put it delicately, received under very dubious circumstances, for certainly these facts ought to have been known to Dame Sibyl and Seigneur Beaumont.

The irony is that she had no need to go through this charade to sell Brecqhou. It was hers to sell anyway without the consent of anybody, for the simple reason that it was not part of the Fief of Sark. Clearly a case of "Oh what a tangled web we weave, when first we practise to deceive".

CHAPTER FORTY-THREE

WAR COMES TO BRECQHOU
1935-1945

In spite of its being Angelo Clarke's life long ambition to own Brecqhou, he did not stay long because on 23rd June 1929, less than four months after purchasing the island, Brecqhou was again offered at auction in London. Twenty-five potential bidders attended, with the opening bid being £25. Bearing in mind that at an auction, the successful bidder is contracted to buy and the vendor is contracted to sell, one wonders what might have happened if, for instance, a German buyer had applied for congé **after** having contractually bought Brecqhou. There was nothing in the auction advertisements which restricted bidders to British subjects. Fortunately, the island was withdrawn at £3,700.

In May 1935, Clarke sold the island to a Captain Tom Clark (no relation) for £3,500. He was a leading member of a wealthy family from Cork engaged in a tobacco business which was eventually acquired by the Imperial Tobacco Company Ltd and Clark's nephew eventually became Chairman of that large concern.

In the thirties, it was not unknown for wealthy men to dress in somewhat shabby attire and Tom Clark was no exception. Indeed, when turning up to inspect Brecqhou he was dressed in a filthy old raincoat and when he offered the estate agent a cigarette, the man was appalled to find the cigarette case filled with half-smoked stubs. It is not recorded whether he accepted!

Clark's influence on Brecqhou was substantial. He built a small jetty and then a house. He installed an aerial ropeway which transported persons, luggage, stores and cattle from the jetty to the plateau. It took two men fifteen months to install, using machinery supplied by Messrs J M Henderson of Aberdeen.

In 1940, Captain Clark decided it would be politic to return to mainland Britain. Clark had obtained his rank in the Munster Fusiliers in the Great War and obviously felt that to remain behind would not be wise. He bought a property near Dartmouth and later, the island of Gruline in Scotland. He died in 1944 and as a consequence of his having acquired a property in the UK, an important and long-running tax case took place in The High Court in Dublin over death duties.

Relocating to the UK was clearly the correct decision because the Germans looted the property on the island. They first visited it in 1940 with the Sark Seneschal when Brecqhou was inhabited by five "hermits". Mr Harry Giles, two brothers named Haneffin, an Alderneyman, Le Bourge and the caretaker A G Lyons. The only radio on the island was so large that the Germans could not confiscate it, so it was left in situ.

Brecqhou was progressively looted throughout the war and a graphic account of the last "loot" is contained in the Von Aufsess Occupation Diary. Freiherr Von Aufsess, Head of Civil Affairs in the German Administration landed on Brecqhou on 29th April 1945. He noted the attempts at afforestaion with saplings protected by up-ended tar barrels. Climbing up to the house he commented that "although the road was only 500 metres long, it gave Captain Clark sufficient excuse to keep three powerful expensive motor-cars on the island". (This does seem to be a bit far-fetched though.) The house had, according to him, been broken into and shamelessly looted with only books remaining, which, he states, one assumes from experience, are the last things to be looted.

However, old Nazi habits die hard, so in spite of the fact that at that date, the war was clearly lost, Von Aufsess "liberated" chairs, curtains, vases and crockery for use in the Standort Kommandantur.

On 2nd June 1944, a US airman was shot down and was in a rubber dinghy off Brecqhou when a Guernsey fisherman rescued him. The survivor was being shot at, presumably by German fighters, but in spite of that, the fisherman recovered the airman and took him to Guernsey. Later on the same day he was summoned to the German Harbour Captain's office to meet an un-named German general who congratulated the fisherman on his bravery and presented him with 100 cigarettes, a bottle of Martell brandy and pouches of tobacco for his deckhands. Apart from the fact that the fisherman was an ex-Merchant Navy captain born on 24th January 1878, nothing more is known of him.

Brecqhou along with Sark and Herm figured in a number of projected and actual attempts to land members of the Special Landing Squadron but no raid on Brecqhou was actually executed. A military file in the Public Record Office at Kew shows a quite remarkable and creditable attempt to cover all eventualities in the matter of pre-raid reconnaissance, with maps, postcards, holidaymakers' snaps and official photographs showing the whole of Sark and Brecqhou even down to the existence of the aerial ropeway on the latter and the statement that "few, if any, houses on Sark have cellars".

CHAPTER FORTY-FOUR

POST-WAR BRECQHOU

In May 1947, an eccentric, monocled ex-officer, Captain Edwin Lawton and his 13 year-old son, landed on Brecqhou with a view to taking it over and growing food thereon. Lawton enlisted the support of his MP Tom Williams. Lawton's letter was a bit peremptory, demanding as it did, advice, tackle and seeds, "at once"!

Island of Brecqhou
Channel Islands
15th April 1947

Tom Williams Esq MP
Sir,

> *I hope you have heard of the Island of Brecqhou, it will, if you have, give more point to my request.*

> *This island is some 160 acres in area, 60 to 70 acres have been cultivated and once produced excellent crops of all kinds but the land has lain fallow since 1941, some of it for a longer period.*

> *I intend, D.V. to get the land in full crop again as soon as possible and to this end, ask for your assistance.*

> *May I ask you to personally give your local officials of the Ministry of Agriculture instructions to give to me (<u>at once</u>, or it will be too late) every assistance within their resources, of advice, tackle and machines in obtaining seed.*

> *In these days I feel sure you will appreciate my anxiety to get weaving and not miss the oportunity of <u>producing food this year.</u>*

I am Sir,
Your obedient servant
Edwin Lawton, Capt

At first, Lawton was assumed to be a prospective purchaser and was left alone, but it soon became clear that he was a trespasser. The Seigneur sent the Prévot over to Brecqhou to tear down notices erected by Lawton and to remove his possessions. Local boatmen were forbidden to transport the pair. Lawton complained to the Home Office about the treatment, but it was pointed out that this was the standard procedure with "squatters".

In the face of such opposition, Lawton and his son slipped quietly away to pastures new. Conceptually, the plan was sound; here was a fairly fertile island, untilled, at a time when every effort was required to feed the nation. However, a trespass had been committed, no matter how worthy the cause.

In 1949, Tom Clark's widow sold Brecqhou for £15,000 to John Thomson Donaldson, one of two reclusive brothers operating in the clothing trade under the brand name of "DonBros". With virtually unlimited resources at his command, Donaldson flooded the island with labourers to set right the neglect of the previous nine years. At the same time, a Jersey farmer, one Charles Talbot, had been given notice to quit his holding and attracted by an advertisement placed by Donaldson, took on the task of farming Brecqhou.

Talbot was the first person to cultivate Brecqhou properly and intensively. He and his wife Ethel grew oats, maize, swedes, potatoes, peas, beans and hay. It was often possible to harvest a crop of new potatoes in the first days of April and surplus potatoes were sent to Guernsey for onward export to the UK. It was reckoned that each cow produced 12 pints of cream each week and the surplus was also sent to Guernsey.

Mrs Donaldson stayed for only one year. She could not stand the sort of existence which was commonplace on the island. Thereafter, she only attended to act as hostess when, each year, the Governor of Guernsey paid his "state" visit.

Suddenly in 1965, after the Labour victory in the mainland election, Donaldson left for Switzerland. Overnight, an island community of 14 persons vanished. Farmer Talbot's ten years of blood, sweat and tears seemed wasted. Fortunately, Leonard Matchan sought him out and offered Talbot and his wife their old cottage and jobs back, which they accepted until 1969 when they retired to Gloucestershire.

CHAPTER FORTY-FIVE

A CHANGE OF TEMPO

1965-1999

The personal flag of Leonard Matchan

Heraldic Description

-Argent, a cross Gules cantoned between the dexter chief a quarter Gules, charged with two lion leopardes (passant gardant) Or, and in sinister base an escutcheon per fess Gules and Or, a fess Vair between, in chief two seagulls in flight Argent in fess and in the base three trefoils slipped Vert-

In March 1966 Leonard Joseph Matchan, founder and Chairman of Cope Allman International Ltd bought the island of

Brecqhou from John Thomson Donaldson for £44,000 plus a small sum for stock and equipment. Prior to that, Matchan had lived at Canford Cliffs near Bournemouth but realised that with the advent of helicopters for personal use, it would be just as quick to travel from Brecqhou to London as it would be from Bournemouth to London. It was also considerably more tax-efficient! Matchan, a Certified Accountant was at one time the European Vice-President of Max Factor. He stood as a Labour candidate in the 1951 election but lost.

Matchan had a modest mansion, La Grande Maison, built on the island by Messrs A E Farr of Westbury, Wilts. The cost was £13,455.2s.4d and it earned the builder the princely profit of £63.1s.3d Although some local stone was used, most came from Portand and Guernsey.

The house had a master suite with attached bathroom and sauna, six other double bedrooms, all en suite, and staff quarters. Furnishings came from two top London stores, and were selected by Matchan's personal assistant Miss Sue Groves.

In 1967, Leonard Matchan decided to have his own flag authorised. Because of his Scottish ancestry, he applied to the Lord Lyon King of Arms who, on 7th July 1967, in a rather splendid recital, extracts of which appear below, approved the new flag which heads this chapter.

"Having considered the same and found that, there being no Court Record at Serq, it was expedient that the Petitioner's flag be placed on record so that Princes and others, by land or sea might have knowledge of the Ensigns Armorial. That the said Leonard Joseph Matchan de Brechou being Sieur de Brechou and vassal in Fief to the Realm of Sercq under a deed from the said Dame of Serq of date 2nd May 1966 in which fief the said Leonard Joseph Matchan had been duly invested as her vassal, the said Ensign Armorial was granted"

Sometime in the 1960's, Leonard Matchan separated from Kathleen, his wife of thirty-odd years and ran away to Brecqhou with Sue Groves. There was never a divorce as it was believed that Mrs

Matchan was strictly opposed to any such thing, so the relationship between Matchan and Sue Groves was never formalised.

In 1986 Leonard Matchan either put Brecqhou on the market, or was approached to do so. The person in question, who must still be referred to as Mr X, was a retired army officer and an ordained priest of the Church of England, and he had "a cunning plan". He wished to buy Brecqhou with a view to allowing Hong Kong Chinese to live there either under a Brecqhou passport or as time spent qualifying for UK residence.

After taking Counsel's opinion he found the plan to be unworkable. Indeed, it is believed that he did not pay any of his advisers, including learned counsel and he eventually went into the Scottish equivalent of bankruptcy with one of the creditors being a finance house who lent £450,000 on a property that subsequently was sold by the lender for £64,000.

However, what is significant is that he was a fairly erudite sort of chap, and he also concluded that Breqchou was not part of Sark. His plan was to pay the Treizième under duress, sue Michael Beaumont for its return and reject the seat in Chief Pleas as being "ultra vires", and of course, he would have been right. Alas, it all came to naught, and the Sarkese lost the possibility of having on their doorstep, one of the great wonders of the 20th century, a Chinese takeaway!

Because unformalised relationships between men and women can often be challenged when one party dies and because of the 30 year age difference between himself and Miss Groves, Leonard Matchan took quite reasonable steps to secure Miss Grove's future should he predecease her. In simple terms, he formed a company, Solaria, and granted it a long lease of Brecqhou. He then presented all of the shares in Solaria to Miss Groves so that she owned and controlled the company which owned the long lease of Brecqhou. She was thus free to stay on Brecqhou after Matchan's death, or assign the lease for a capital sum if she wished to live elsewhere.

Believing, erroneously, that Brecqhou was part of the Fief of

Sark, Matchan submitted the lease to the Sark Greffier for registration in the Greffe Office records. The Greffier, J P Hamon, was reluctant at first to register the lease until the Seigneur had an opportunity to read the conditions. However, Hamon wrote to Carey Langlois, Advocates of Guernsey on 18th December 1987 as follows:

"I return herewith the Lease of the island of Brecqhou <u>duly registered on the Records of the island of Sark.</u>

I approached the Seigneur regarding this lease and felt that due to the conditions laid down in the Contract that it would be advisable he be made aware of the contents of the Contract therefore after you have perused the Contract, copy enclosed, I hope you will appreciate my reluctance to register this lease <u>before obtaining the consent and permission of the Seigneur.</u>"

<u>*(The underlining is the author's)*</u>

(Incidentally, Matchan died on 6th October 1987).

It would be difficult to ask for a more unambiguous letter.

Out of the woodwork came Peter Matchan, Leonard's only son. Embittered by the treatment meted out to his mother and by his father's often-stated remark that he (Peter) would never inherit a single penny, Matchan junior commenced an action in the Sark Court to recover ownership of Brecqhou and to have the Solaria lease set aside.

At this point the matter took an interesting turn. John Michael Beaumont, Seigneur of Sark, entered the fray and is reported as making the following statement to a Sunday newspaper:

"Under our laws land always goes to the son. If everybody did what Leonard Matchan has done the islands would just fall apart."

What was it Leonard Matchan had done that so upset John Michael Beaumont? Why, he had granted a long lease of his freehold island to Solaria Investments Limited. Who, according to the Greffier, had studied the terms and then approved registration of the lease? Why, the very same John Michael Beaumont, Seigneur of Sark.

Miss Groves gave instructions for the case to be vigorously defended. Given that the plaintiff, Peter Matchan, had the Seigneur of Sark on his side, there ought to have been a speedy resolution to this case. After all, the defendant, Miss Sue Groves, was on her own, very much the "other woman", had no legal standing vis-à-vis the deceased Leonard Matchan and ought to have been a "pushover".

However the case dragged on for six years and in the end, Miss Groves, because of ill-health, threw in the towel and settled out of Court. One can only speculate as to why a simple dispute, which ought to have been dispatched by a Court very quickly, never got beyond a rather comic instant adjournment in the Sark Court. The theory is that once Miss Groves started to pursue the question of whether or not Brecqhou was part of the Fief of Sark rather than answer the spurious charges brought by Peter Matchan, the case had to be delayed because an appearance in court on those grounds would have opened a very nasty can of worms going back to 1928.

Brecqhou, held by Solaria Investments by lease and thus in effect, wholly owned by Miss Groves, was adjudged to be worth about £3.5m. Since that is the approximate price reported to have been paid by the Barclays, that must have represented the open market value. There is no Treizième payable on the grant or assignment of a Sark lease, so the sale of the lease of Brecqhou would not have benefited the Seigneur in any way. If it were possible to have the lease set aside, then Peter Matchan would have been able to sell the island as a freehold and John Michael Beaumont would have recieved a Treizième.

Out of the settlement, Peter Matchan received £2.3 million for the "freehold" and Miss Groves £1.2 million for her lease. John Michael Beaumont, Seigneur of Sark, collected a Treizième of nearly £180,000. It was rumoured on Sark that the day after receiving the Treizième, Mrs Beaumont went to Guernsey to book a world cruise!

One of the allegations which appeared in the summons served by Peter Matchan on Miss Groves was the statement:

"the lease being a sale or alienation within the said conditions or

stipulations was made without the express permission or licence of the Seigneur of Sark."

Yet, as demonstrated previously, it appears from the Sark court records that Seigneur Beaumont knew full well the import of the Solaria lease and approved it.

Another allegation was:

"under Sark Law an inheritor is entitled to take such inheritance free of encumbrance and in the circumstance, the lease is an encumbrance."

Yet in 1963-1964 correspondence passed between Mrs Bell, the Deputy Dame and Procureur Loveridge setting out quite cogently that a lease was not an encumbrance. It is thought unlikely that Mrs Bell would have omitted to place these papers into the Seigneurie records as a fundamental interpretation of Sark Law. Since they have been quoted in a recent case, they would also appear to have been freely available in 1987 to the present Seigneur and his advisers when they challenged Miss Groves.

Miss Groves lost out by approximately £2.3 million. In 1991, in the Sark case of Baker v Dewe, an heiress tried to have a long lease set aside on the grounds that it contained no rent reviews. She lost her case and the lease had to stand, "as written". These records exist in the Sark Greffe Office to this day. The Solaria lease was legal and this fact should have been known when Miss Groves settled her litigation. The point had also been raised many times by Dame Sibyl Hathaway since 1928 when she tried to break an earlier Brecqhou lease merely because it had not been registered at the Greffe Office on Sark.

According to Seigneur Beaumont, the lease was illegal. Thus Solaria ought to have received nothing for the lease, and Peter Matchan should have received £3.5 million for the freehold. In fact, the former's share was £1.2 million and the latter's £2.3 million. How could this compromise be justified if the laws of primogeniture were observed punctiliously?

More to the point, what authority did Mr Beaumont have, as Seigneur of Sark, to bend the laws he so jealousy guards? The Solaria lease was either legal or illegal. It could not be one third legal and two thirds illegal! For Solaria to have received even one penny for the lease is a de facto recognition that it was legal. It therefore follows that Solaria should have received the full £3.5 million.

THE POSTAL HISTORY OF BRECQHOU LASTED FOR PRECISELY ONE DAY!

In September 1969, the Owner of Brecqhou, Leonard Matchan, planned and executed an issue of stamps for the Island he owned. More properly called "carriage labels" they were
ostensibly issued to pay for the cost of delivering letters to a recognised General Post Office, in this case, Guernsey. In all 25,000 sets of stamps were issued, of which 10,000
were used on First Day Covers.

Leonard Matchan used the older spelling of Brecqhou on his stamps.

The day after the issue, stamps of Brecqhou were suppressed by the Guernsey Postal
Authority when they took over responsibility from the United Kingdom for the issue of
postage stamps.

CHAPTER FORTY-SIX

ENTER THE BARCLAYS

The purchasers of Brecqhou in 1993 were David and Frederick Barclay, the reclusive millionaire twins who seem to have picked up the baton relinquished by Miss Groves and who, at the time of writing, are believed to be pursuing the case of Brecqhou in the Royal Court of Guernsey and the European Court of Human Rights.

Probably as a result of the Groves case, the Barclays were required to have included in the purchase deed, the following statement:

"The island of Brecqhou forms part of Sark and remains under the jurisdiction of Sark and the laws and usages and customs of Sark extend and apply there as of right."

Such a condition was wholly unprecedented and has never been used in the transfer of any other Sark Tenement. Both buyer and seller had everything arranged to complete and the requirement for this new paragraph was presented at the last moment. Indeed, it could be said to have been submitted under duress. Such a declaration has no validity in law. One could insert a clause that a certain piece of land in Guernsey comes under the laws of France, but this has no meaning if the historical facts point otherwise. It does however seem to demonstrate the reluctance of Seigneur Beaumont to admit that he might possibly be wrong about Brecqhou.

There was, and is, no precedent for applying Sark Law to

Brecqhou. Sark bans the landing of aircraft, the keeping of bitches and the use of motor vehicles. In the time of Leonard Matchan, he kept bitches, flew a helicopter into and out of Brecqhou and drove around his small island in a Land Rover. There are no recorded instances of the Constable and Vingtenier together with members of the Guernsey Constabulary landing on Brecqhou to enforce Sark Law.

Once the Barclay brothers made it known that they were going to challenge the title of Brecqhou, they were subject to what can only be described as harassment by the Sark authorities. In November 1995, the Constable and Vingtenier of Sark, together with a detective sergeant from Guernsey made an unprecedented "official" visit to Brecqhou. Their pretext was to check pony registration and gun licences. The fact that they were told that there were no guns on the island and that there was no legal requirement to register ponies in Brecqhou or Sark anyway, did not seem to matter.

The Constable then expressed concern that the large number of workmen on Brecqhou (engaged in the construction of the Barclays' residence) did not have work permits. Again, the fact that there is no requirement under Sark or European Law for work permits for citizens of the EU, did not seem to cut any ice. During the visit, the Constable produced a copy of an employment form for the island of Sark which, it transpired, had no legal basis either on Brecqhou or Sark.

A further and more serious attempt at harassment was made in February 1996. A construction worker on Brecqhou was found to be in possession of drugs for his personal use. The building contractors dismissed him and handed him over to HM Customs & Excise in Guernsey; so far, the behaviour one would expect from responsible employers.

The next day, Customs hauled him back to Sark where he was arrested by the Sark Constable and tried by the Seneschal without any legal representation. The case was conducted partly in French and was unintelligible to the accused. On the advice of a Guernsey advocate he pleaded guilty and was fined £300 and returned to Guernsey. It is interesting to consider whether the action of HM Customs here was correct. To extradite an offender to another jurisdiction without any enquiry as to the propriety of doing so, seems inequitable, even if the offence involved drugs.

Who put the Constable up to this? It is not thought for one moment that the officer, one Roger Knight, woke up one day and said to his assistant, "What a grand day for turning over Brecqhou". No unpaid constables are voluntarily going to take on an island full of brawny builders and labourers. It seems obvious that orders came down from on high for them to become involved. Then a very curious thing happened. The Constable vanished!

Around 21st March 1996, Roger Knight left Sark to visit his parents in London. According to newspaper reports, he was never heard of again. Rumours circulated around Sark that a large amount of money vanished with him. It was reported he was seen penniless on the streets of New York. Was he pushed, or did he go of his own accord? Perhaps he could not stomach being involved in harassing the Barclay brothers.

Undoubtedly the Barclays will win not as many will suggest, because they have the might and that might is right but because of historical truth. However, they may not now need to pursue their case in the Guernsey Court because the recently decided case of de Carteret v Surcouf has opened the door to the creation of an underlease to Brecqhou in favour of whomsoever the Barclays choose.

To be fair, until some four years ago, the author would not have countenanced any suggestion that Brecqhou was not part of Sark. The two islands seemed totally entwined. However, as the late Professor Joad would have said, "It all depends what you mean by 'part of'."

Harassment from Sark still goes on at sporadic intervals. Complaints about the Barclays' helicopter continue to be made although nothing is said when the same helicopter is used to assist Sark. A suggestion was made that a plane should fly over Brecqhou to take photographs to examine any buildings erected without planning permission, quite ignoring the fact that Sark has no jurisdiction over the island.

Curiously enough the name Barclay comes from Roger de Berchelai, who accompanied William the Conqueror to Hastings. One branch of that family became the Berkeleys of Gloucester and the other branch wandered into Scotland and became Lairds of Towrie. It could be said that the Barclay brothers, having roots going back to Normandy and the Channel Islands, are only reclaiming their inheritance.

It seems clear that the de Carterets knew that Brecqhou was not part of the Fief of Sark. The Le Pelleys undoubtedly knew it. William A Toplis, the artist, certainly knew it. Dame Sibyl Hathaway decidedly knew it. Miss Groves knew it. Mr X reckoned to know it. It is hoped that after reading this section of the book, you, the reader, will be in no doubt. The facts are so conclusive. During the research done for this book, not a single shred of evidence came to light which placed Brecqhou into the Fief of Sark. Such a paucity of evidence is unusual, for invariably one stumbles across a document which may substantiate the opposite view or at least cause one to stop and re-evaluate one's data. No such documents have emerged, not even a single sentence which might have made the author have a fleeting second thought.

CHAPTER FORTY-SEVEN

THE OWNERS OF BRECQHOU

EPILOGUE

In the sixteenth century,
way ahead of his time,
Helier de Carteret
had created the perfect democracy in Sark
under the guise of a feudal state.

By the end of the nineteenth century Sark,
still ahead of the times,
had degenerated into the first of Europe's facist
dictatorships under the
control of one extended family.

(From the Biography of William A Toplis by Paul A Toplis)

BIBLIOGRAPHY

Axton, Dr Richard: *A Portrait of Guernsey*

Beaumont, J M: *The Consitution and Administration of Sark*

Bell William M: *I beg to Report and The Commando Who Came Home To Spy*

Bloch, Marc: *Feudal Society*

Cruickshank, Charles: *The German Occupation of the Channel Islands*

De Carteret & Ewen: *The Fief of Sark*

Falby, Douglas: *The Island of Brecqhou (unpublished)*

Gurney, David: *The Post Office in the Smaller Channel Islands*

Hathaway, Sibyl: *Dame of Sark*

Hakes, Ken: *Sark*

Hurden, Bethia J: *The Royal Sark Militia*

Jamieson, A G (and others): *A People of the Sea*

Marr, L James: *A History of the Bailiwick of Guernsey*

Stoney, Barbara: *Sibyl, Dame of Sark*

Tremayne, Julia: *War on Sark - Diaries of Julia Tremayne*

Toplis, Paul: *William A Toplis, Artist of Sark*

Utley, John: *The Story of the Channel Islands*

Von Aufsess: *Von Aufsess Occupation Diaries*

Wearis, F: *News from the Channel*

GLOSSARY

Seneschal: *The Lord's Steward. Generally has some legal knowledge and acts as a Judge at the Manorial courts.*

Constable: *Unpaid voluntary law officer who, on Sark serves for one year before being replaced by the Vingtenier.*

Vingtenier: *Originally the tithing man. Now acts as deputy Constable on Sark before taking the latter's position after one year.*

Tithes: *One tenth of certain products which were due to the Lord of the Manor. Cereals etc. are known as the "great tithes", other items known as "small tithes". (Also known as dîmes, or dismes)*

Clameur de Haro: *A Norman form of injunction whereby the instigator by using a set procedure and uttering certain words and prayers, causes instant cessation of the illegal acts of another.*

Seigneur: *The Norman equivalent to Lord of the Manor.*

Seigneurie: *The residence of the Seigneur.*

Chief Pleas: *The Parliament of Sark.*

Tenants: *The owners of the forty original Tenements of Sark.*

Tenements: *The forty original sub-divisions of the land area of Sark as decided by Helier de Carteret in 1565.*

Prévot: *Officer of the Sark Court who executes judgements, the Sheriff.*

Greffier: *Clerk of the Sark Court who records the decisions of the Court.*

Greffe Office: *The office wherein is kept all details of judgements etc. of the Sark Court and where leases and other documents are registered.*

Douzaine: *Persons elected by Chief Pleas from amongst members of that body, to enforce or oversee certain administrative duties.*

Retraite: *Upon the sale of real property, members of the seller's family within certain "degrees of affinity" have the right to purchase for themselves, the said* property within one year and one day, by paying to the original purchaser, the consideration and his expenses.

Escheat: *Where a Tenant dies and there are no heirs to within 7 degrees of affinity, the property reverts to the Lord of the Manor as his own property.*

Primogeniture: *A system of inheritance whereby real estate devolves only to the eldest son upon the death of the father.*

Treizième: *A fraction of the purchase price which is paid to the Seigneur for grant of conge. This amount is for the Seigneur's own pocket. On Sark the fraction is one thirteenth of the purchase consideration.*

Congé: *The grant, by the Seigneur, of permission to purchase real estate on Sark.*

Ordinance: *A local law.*

Impot: *Import tax or duty.*

Knight's fee: *A measure of personal service to the Crown. Can involve a maximum of forty days service under arms for a "full knight". Later commuted for money rather than actual physical service. Knight's service was given in a exchange for the grant of real estate.*

Fief: *The area under the direct control and ownership of a Lord or Seigneur.*

Fief Haubert: *The highest form of knight service, representing 40 days military service given to the Crown. In france, such an honour was indicated by wearing a suit of chain mail.*

Corvée: *A traditional system, once prevalent in western Europe, whereby road repairs were shared between inhabitants pro-rata their land ownership.*

Letters Patent: *Documents issued by the Crown on many subjects including grants of land, appointments of Commissioners, gifts of property and title, sealed with the Great Seal of England and representing in effect, the executive order of the Monarch.*

Livres Tournois: *A method of reckoning evolved from the time the English occupied the French city of Tours. The rate of exchange varies but around 1850. was 14 Livres/pounds tournois to £1 sterling.*